The Yellowstone National Park

Cookbook

by Durrae Johanek

RIVERBEND
PUBLISHING

D1637260

To my husband, John … Just because.

Cover and text design by DD Dowden
ISBN 10: 1-931832-78-1
ISBN 13: 978-1-931832-78-6

RIVERBEND PUBLISHING
P.O. Box 5833
Helena, MT 59604
Toll-free 1-866-787-2363
www.riverbendpublishing.com

Contents

Acknowledgments

A sincere thank you goes to all who helped me make contacts, get permissions, or in any way assisted in getting *The Yellowstone National Park Cookbook* into print: Sandra Bockman of the Jackson Chamber of Commerce, Jack and Sue Davis, Cristin Dhieux-Bray, Katie Duffy, Jillian and Parker Fink, Jim Fowler, Lou Harlow, Rick Hoeninghausen, Jim Horan, Erica Hutchings, Jan Laye, Tom Mesereau, Leslie and Ruth Quinn, Dave Reetz of the Cody Chamber of Commerce, Lee Whittlesey, and Ryan Yeager.

Special thanks go to Lois Blasberg, who deciphered handwritten recipes and keyed them in, with no errors, an amazing feat in this typing-challenged author's eyes, and to Bonnie Murphy, who allowed me to use recipes from her own book, *Bonnie Cooks*. And without my husband's constructive criticism, *The Yellowstone National Park Cookbook* would have been just another book.

Introduction

· · · · · · · · · · · · · · · · · · · ·

"Wonderland" is Yellowstone National Park's nickname. Some people use it as their email address, sport it on personalized license plates, embroider it on their favorite wolf-watching hat—anywhere they can think to advertise their passion for the nation's first national park. Other folks are more subtle—they moved to Montana, Wyoming, or Idaho to be near Yellowstone. They're especially lucky and they know it.

The Yellowstone National Park Cookbook is about these people, whether employees or visiting devotees. Barbara Forbes Rinker was a Yellowstone savage and proud of it. Jack Gilchrist looks forward to meeting his buddies in Lamar for a hearty day of bear watching. As park superintendent, Suzanne Lewis is a very busy person—period. There is little if anything park historian Lee Whittlesey doesn't know about Yellowstone's history. The list goes on….

In addition to learning about the people behind the recipes in this book, you'll pick up some park history. For example, Dianna Kellie—whose goal is to stay in every room in Old Faithful Inn—tells how August 25 came to be Christmas in Yellowstone. On that date in 1910 visitors were stranded by a snowstorm. Instead of mass panic, someone thought it would be a good idea to ease the tension by putting up a Christmas tree and celebrating the snow. Visitors now plan their trips around that date to exchange gifts, decorate their rooms, and sing Christmas carols around the piano. And where else would Santa come down a Crow's Nest?

Tour leader Leslie Quinn has the answer to what fuels the passion for Yellowstone, what it is about the park that makes people change their lives to live near it or in it. "Montana and Wyoming are still very wild places but even there, in nearly any town, you can find what you need or don't need—wireless Internet, malls, chain stores, etcetera," he says. "But when you get inside the park, there are places where you can have a view of 15 to 20 miles in any direction without any light or human structure. To walk in the backcountry you know you're in the presence of wildness—there's a thrill to that." Not to mention it is comfort food for the soul.

Even the recipes in *The Yellowstone National Park Cookbook* have history. Many of them are passed down among friends and family with directions that would make Emeril weep. But that's their charm (although I did try to retain the original wording as much as possible). One can only assume that a "moderate oven" is 325 to 350 degrees and that the measurement of "butter the size of a walnut" is clear to the reader. And just try to find Hershey bars at five cents each for Bob Richard's Whistle Creek Almond Roca.

The recipes run the gamut from handy backpacking foods to gourmet meals from the park restaurants to munchies for vegetarians to wild game stews and entrees. Some of the recipes include how-to's, recipe backgrounds, and do's and don'ts (the italic text comes from the recipe owner; the other suggestions are mine).

An additional bonus to *The Yellowstone National Park Cookbook* is the websites mentioned in the profiles. On the GOSA site Old Faithful geyser erupts on your desktop via a webcam or you can monitor geyser eruptions throughout the world. You'll also learn how geyser gazers are helping to preserve thermal features. Shop for park-related books and other items at the Yellowstone Association's website—www.yellowstoneassociation.org—or better yet, become a member. Need a blue-ribbon guide for just about anything? Check out Bob Richard's site. Photography? Tom Murphy is the go-to guy. For pure nostalgia, visit Barbara Forbes Rinker's site—you'll be humming "Edelweiss" for days.

Whether you bought this book for its recipes, the profiles, or just because there wasn't a Yellowstone T-shirt in your size, you now own not only some great food ideas but also an insight into the park's history, its people, its wildlife, and its thermal features.

A wonderland? You betcha.

Breakfast

Five Species Marmalade

. . . .

Jennifer Whipple

As a botanist, I can't help but be intrigued with all of the species of citrus fruit that are available. After a trip to Britain, I developed a taste for marmalade so I started to experiment with different citrus fruits, especially kumquats, a favorite of Ruthie, my "aunt" who was my mentor as a wildflower enthusiast.

10 to 12 kumquats
1 mandarin orange (such as Satsuma)
2 limes
2 lemons
2 oranges
Sugar
Water

Scrub the fruit, cut in half, remove the seeds, and *thinly* slice the fruit into very small pieces. Measure the fruit and juice and add three times the amount of water (the recipe can be doubled if you want to make more marmalade). Soak for 12 hours. Simmer about 20 minutes, then let stand again for another 12 hours.

For every cup of fruit and juice add ¾ cup of sugar. In a large pot, bring 4 to 6 cups of the fruit, water, and sugar mixture to boil (don't use more than 6 cups at one time!). Cook until the mixture reaches the "sheeting stage," when the syrup thickens and the separate drops come together and form a single glob.

Meanwhile, have sterilized jars and lids ready. Keep the jars in hot or boiling water until ready, then take out of the water, turn upright, and fill with the jam immediately when it is at the proper sheeting stage to form a jelly. Place lids on the jars, screw on the lids, then turn quickly upside down, and then place right side up to cool.

Jennifer Whipple, *Park Botanist*

Her answering machine says: "This is Jennifer Whipple in the herbarium. It is the summer field season and I'm a moving target—feel free to leave a message but I can't tell you when I'm going to get it."

Before one questions just how busy can a botanist be, note that Yellowstone hosts 1,200 to 1,300 species of flowering plants, all of which are part of a huge ecosystem and all, like everything in the park, under its protection. Jen notes that you can't keep anything from the park—you can get fined, and she won't hesitate to give you a warning if she sees you with a handful of park flowers. "Most people understand, and I take it as an opportunity to teach." For those who want more information, Jen offers a course at the Yellowstone Institute in early June on spring wildflowers.

Jen's interest in plants was cultivated while in junior high school in California when she couldn't identify wildflowers behind her house. They weren't in a typical field guide because they were growing on a type of rock inhospitable to plants. When she finally figured out what they were, she was hooked. She says, "One nice thing about plants is they don't fly away—making them easier to identify. Also nice is that you can travel a very short distance and have some different species to investigate."

Finding a new species can make any botanist positively giddy but that happens more infrequently than Jen would like. More commonly her job is conducting rare plant surveys. With constant roadwork needed to accommodate millions of tourists, surveys help make sure no plants of concern are destroyed in road construction or maintenance. "We carefully remove the topsoil, then put it back after the road is finished, thus preserving the seed bank." But not everything that grows in Yellowstone is wanted. Noxious weeds such as leafy spurge and spotted knapweed are a concern. "For example, leafy spurge roots can reach as much as 30 feet down, which is a problem because they can take over and result in monocultures of noxious weeds that are unpalatable to wildlife."

Park visitors can see evidence of the fires of 1988 and some visitors may be aware that certain tree species need fire to reproduce, but Jen enthusiastically describes a flower that is totally dependent on fire: Bicknell's geranium. "I'd never seen Bicknell's in the park, but in 1989 rosettes were all over the place. They overwintered and produced profuse blooms the following year—it was solid Bicknell's. Now the seed is sitting in the ground waiting for the next fire."

Jen has little time to share her knowledge in print but she is one of the authors of and has contributed her photography to the *Wyoming Rare Plant Field Guide*. "I'd love to write a book on park flora for the general public, but that's down the road," she sighs.

This busy botanist will gladly answer any of your questions on Yellowstone's flora, but she can be tough to nail down—"feel free to leave a message."

Recipes by Jennifer Whipple

Old Faithful Scones

Jennifer Whipple

While living at Old Faithful during the winter, there was no easy source of baked goods. After much experimentation, I developed these breakfast scones for a snowy winter day.

4 cups flour
$1/2$ cup sugar
1 teaspoon salt
4 teaspoons baking powder
1 teaspoon cinnamon
$1/2$ teaspoon nutmeg
$1/2$ cup butter
$1^1/2$ teaspoons orange rind, grated
2 eggs
1 cup milk (I use skim)
1 cup raisins

Mix flour, sugar, salt, baking powder, cinnamon, and nutmeg. Add butter and cut it in until the mixture resembles coarse cornmeal. Cut in the orange rind. Beat eggs lightly in separate bowl and add milk. Add liquid mixture into the dry ingredients (make a shallow hole in the center of the dry mixture) along with the raisins. Stir just until everything is moistened and almost totally mixed.

Take dough onto counter or breadboard, and fold and knead two or three times to finish mixing all the ingredients together. Cut the dough into squares about 2 inches across, and place well apart on cookie sheet. Lightly moisten surface of scones with a little milk and dust with a cinnamon/sugar mixture (1 teaspoon cinnamon for $1/2$ cup sugar).

Bake at 425º for 10 to 12 minutes.

Phonograph's Sourdough Sponge & Hotcakes

Bob Richard

On trips to Yellowstone, Phonograph Jones would whip up his specialty for the guests.

Sourdough sponge:

    2 cups warm water
    2 yeast cakes (add more if necessary)
    1/2 cup sugar
    2 cups flour

Stir and let sit for two days (about 48 hours) in a warm area.

To make hotcakes:

Add to sourdough sponge:

    1 cup water
    1 cup flour
    4 tablespoons shortening
    3 to 4 tablespoons sugar as necessary
    1 teaspoon baking soda
    1 teaspoon salt
    3 to 5 eggs

Cook on hot griddle.

Special Butter for Hotcakes & Waffles

You can ease up on the cinnamon if you want a milder taste, but don't do away with it entirely— it really makes the butter taste good.

    1 pound butter
    1 1/2 cups brown sugar
    1 tablespoon cinnamon, or to taste
    1/2 teaspoon vanilla

Whip it together.

Sarah's Hot Granola

Walter Voeller

This is a good backpacking meal. You can vary the granola and fixin's but this cereal comes presweetened (generally) so there's one less thing to bring.

General hot cereal recipe:

1 part granola
1^1/$_2$ parts water or water and milk mixed
Fruit
Butter, optional
Whipping cream, optional

Stir and cook cereal 3 to 5 minutes.

I usually add raisins, but craisins, dried mango, fresh apples, bananas are good, too. Serve with butter and whipping cream if "going in style."

Scotch Eggs

. . . .

Ruth & Leslie Quinn

This is a good dish to make with a companion—you may want to have someone handy to turn on the water for you to wash your hands because they will be sticky and caked with crumbs.

13 large eggs
2 pounds ground pork sausage
1 cup crushed whole-wheat crackers

Boil 12 eggs for about 12 minutes. Once the eggs have drained and cooled, peel them and set aside. Cut sausage into 12 equal portions.

Using a fork, beat the last egg in a small bowl. In a larger bowl, crush the crackers—smaller pieces are better.

Roll up your sleeves—it's about to get messy. Take one portion of the sausage, press it between your palms, forming into a thin bowl. The sausage will warm a little as you work with it. Wrap the sausage around one hard-boiled egg until the egg is completely covered. Roll this in the raw egg. Roll in the cracker crumbs to completely cover the surface. Repeat 11 more times, arranging the eggs in a 9 x 12 baking pan.

Bake in a 400° oven for 1 hour, turning the eggs every 15 minutes to cook on all sides. Eat them warm out of the oven, then enjoy them for several days served cold for breakfast.

Ruth & Leslie Quinn, Tour Leaders Extraordinaire

There was a professor in Pennsylvania who could rattle off the date of any event in our country's history.

Yellowstone's Ruth and Leslie Quinn make him look positively amnesic. Leslie's every sentence is punctuated with dates, places, and names, and Ruth can match him fact for fact. Good thing, too, because both are responsible for the information visitors take away from Yellowstone. Leslie teaches all the tour bus drivers not only how to maneuver the buses but also how to share their knowledge of the park with the public—everything from thermal features to wildlife. He even trained Ruth, who, four times a day, four days a week, now leads tours of Old Faithful Inn.

Ruth, a trained social worker from Kansas, and Leslie, with a physics degree from Massachusetts, met in Yellowstone. Leslie left to get his master's in education but after teaching half a year, he hated being away from the park and came back for good.

Ruth's tours and nine years of research led to her labor of love: *Weaver of Dreams,* a major volume on Robert Reamer, the designer of Old Faithful Inn. "I didn't start out to write a book—it was a story I felt had to be told and I was in the position to do that as a tour guide of the inn. All kinds of questions arose about Reamer that we didn't know how to answer."

Ruth feeds off the energy and excitement of the people who are seeing the inn for the first time. "The building interests so many people on so many different levels—from the antique rustic furniture to its construction, its history, even its spirituality." Before the inn, park hotels were built to resemble those in cities to encourage tourists to visit what they considered wild, unsafe places. Reamer's Old Faithful set the standard for today's "parkitecture." During the off season the Quinns are homeless and unemployed. Because their jobs are seasonal, they get bounced out of their housing and stay in local motels or hit the road, knowing that when they get back their jobs will be there. "We love it. We travel, visit friends and family, and once spent 10 days at the national archives in Maryland—an incredible place," says Leslie. "You can't do that with a traditional job."

Leslie *is* a national archive—his head holds more data than most people learn in a lifetime. He throws out, for example, these facts:

- At five million acres Adirondack State Park in New York is larger than Yellowstone.

- The United States invented national parks— they are our great legacy to the world.

- Yellowstone is the world's first and oldest national park but not the largest; a park in Greenland is 77 times larger.

That's just the tip of the Quinns' information iceberg. This couple deserves their own book, but in the meantime tourists will have to be content to take a tour to pick the brains of Ruth and Leslie Quinn.

Recipes by Ruth & Leslie Quinn

Sheehan Pancakes (or waffles)

Carl Sheehan

2 cups buttermilk
1 tablespoon vegetable oil
2 tablespoons apple butter
1 tablespoon brown sugar
$^1/_2$ teaspoon vanilla
$^1/_4$ cup cornmeal
$^1/_4$ cup white flour
$^2/_3$ cup whole-wheat flour
$^1/_4$ cup oatmeal
2 tablespoons wheat germ
$^1/_2$ teaspoon cinnamon
$^1/_2$ teaspoon salt
1 teaspoon baking soda
3 egg whites

Mix in large bowl, buttermilk, vegetable oil, apple butter, brown sugar, and vanilla.

Mix in small bowl, cornmeal, white flour, whole-wheat flour, oatmeal, wheat germ, cinnamon, salt, and baking soda. (Note: if making waffles reduce baking soda to $^1/_2$ teaspoon and add $^1/_2$ teaspoon baking powder.)

In another small bowl beat 3 egg whites. Add dry ingredients to liquid. Fold in egg whites.

If desired, drop berries or nuts on pancakes/waffles while cooking them.

Swedish Pancakes

Tom & Bonnie Murphy

These come from my grandmother in Iowa.

4 eggs
4 tablespoons sugar
1 teaspoon salt
1 cup flour
2 cups milk
4 tablespoons melted butter

In a blender or large bowl, beat together the eggs, sugar, salt, and flour. Beat in the milk until well blended. Melt the butter (do not substitute margarine) and add to the batter, beating thoroughly.

Pour onto a hot, large, cast-iron pancake griddle until griddle is covered thinly, and bake about a minute. Flip over and bake on the other side for half a minute or so.

Roll up and serve with homemade syrup.

Tom & Bonnie Murphy, Photography Expeditions

On a hillside in Yellowstone, camera nearby, Tom Murphy sits, waits, and watches—he's hard at work, listening and observing, and encouraging his tour group to do the same. On today's outing he's working with several photographers, showing them the best angle, lighting, and subject matter and telling them to "watch what goes on under your shoelaces—not everything is on the horizon." He's been doling out this advice since the late 1980s when "there were outfitters for hunting and fishing, but no one had heard of being led on photo tours." So Tom, who never shot a photo until he was 22, became the first photographer licensed to guide photo trips in the park. He says, "People stuck their necks out to come to this place with an unknown photographer at the time. Now they come from all over the world."

Like so many people, Tom and his wife Bonnie fell in love with Yellowstone and moved to Livingston, Montana, where Bonnie worked with emotionally disturbed children and Tom tried to make a living shooting portraits and weddings and leading an occasional day trip tour into the park. One of his photography clients was so impressed with Tom's ability and knowledge of Yellowstone that he cosigned a loan to start Wilderness Photography Expeditions. It went national, then international, but Tom's focus remained on the park. Soon Bonnie quit her job to be the "make-nice lady and cook," Tom says. "Bonnie would show up with hot soup and fresh bread and meet us in the middle of nowhere." Former clients would send her recipes to use, so the light bulb went on and she decided to write a cookbook, *Bonnie Cooks*.

Tom's experience, with a little luck thrown in, has kept backcountry disasters to almost nil. "Nothing major, but one young fellow took a header down a steep slope, landing on his face and breaking his jaw. I have search and rescue medical training and we got him back to Mammoth—he recovered nicely." As for luck, Tom once guided an MTV project that featured

Cameron Diaz and he jokingly recalls that he shared a hot-pot soak with Cameron, but he actually gets more excited about watching pronghorns give birth, a rare event.

Tours have changed. Much of the photography is digital, which often finds Tom in front of a computer, but "the upside is that you get instant feedback and can finesse the final image." Now he has hooked up with resorts that supply the clients and the food (Tom still leads select individual day trips on his own). Bonnie manages www.tmurphywild.com and handles their products—books, DVDs, greeting cards, and prints. Tom's books include the award-winning *Silence & Solitude: Yellowstone's Winter Wilderness* and two titles in his beautiful series, Seasons of Yellowstone.

Tom strongly believes in giving back to the community and wants to garner as many fans for the park as possible. "People have come here and then gone home as serious supporters of Yellowstone, which is really satisfying," he says. "I'll probably do this until I can't walk anymore."

Recipes by Tom & Bonnie Murphy

Zucchini Pancakes

. . . .

Cheryl Jaworowski

*As an avid organic gardener, it seems as if I always need recipes that use zucchini even if
I only have one healthy plant. Zucchini pancakes freeze well and are a good snack.*

1 egg
1 cup milk
$^{1}/_{4}$ cup orange juice
1 cup unbleached flour
1 teaspoon baking powder
1 teaspoon salt
1 cup grated zucchini
2 tablespoons olive or canola oil

Mix egg, milk, and orange juice together. Mix flour, baking powder, and salt together with a fork. Combine wet mixture with dry mixture. Stir in the grated zucchini.

Heat frying pan until small drop of pancake batter beads up. Use a ladle to place pancake batter into frying pan and cook on medium heat. Flip pancakes when bubbles in pancake batter come to the surface and pop.

Serve with chokecherry syrup (homemade or purchased).

As a variation, try adding grated Parmesan cheese or fresh or dried basil.

Breads

Bob's Ranch Biscuits

Bob Richard

1 egg, beaten
1 cube of butter (2 to 3 tablespoons)
2 cups flour
3 tablespoons sugar
$1/2$ teaspoon salt
4 teaspoons baking powder
$1/2$ teaspoon cream of tartar
$3/4$ to 1 cup milk

Preheat oven to 450º.

Combine egg and butter. In separate bowl combine flour, sugar, salt, baking powder, and cream of tartar. Knife dry mixture into egg and butter bowl. Add milk.

Use teaspoon and drop onto greased pan or into Dutch oven. Bake for 10 to 15 minutes or until brown.

Lefse

. . . .

Tom & Bonnie Murphy

Lefse is a Scandinavian staple that resembles a crepe.
It is said that Norwegians will eat fenceposts if you put enough butter on them, and lefse is no exception.
Although it may seem like sacrilege, besides butter and sugar lefse is also good with honey,
peanut butter and jelly, whipped cream—just about anything that suits your fancy.

5 cups mashed potatoes
Milk as needed
1 teaspoon salt
1 tablespoon butter
3 cups flour

Mash the potatoes with the milk, salt, and butter. While mashed potatoes are still warm, add the flour and mix well. Roll out small balls of dough very thin, and bake on a hot, dry grill or in a frying pan on the stovetop.

Letha's Rolls

. . . .

Barbara Forbes Rinker

Letha Forbes, my mother, always made these for Thanksgiving and Christmas dinners.

$1/2$ cup of sugar
1 tablespoon salt
4 tablespoons Crisco
1 cup hot water
1 cup cold water
2 eggs, well beaten
2 cakes yeast dissolved in
  $1/4$ cup of lukewarm water
$61/2$ cups flour

Combine sugar, salt, and Crisco. Add hot water, then cold water; add eggs. Add yeast mixture and flour. Place in greased bowl and cover with wet cloth. Place in refrigerator; use as needed.

In a muffin pan, place 3 small balls of dough in each muffin slot; put a pat of butter on each roll. Bake at 350º for 15 minutes.

Mother's Bread

. . . .

Lee Whittlesey

Lee cherishes his mother's pages-falling-out, food-stained cookbook filled with recipes he enjoyed as a boy. The cookbook is worthy of inducting into the park's archives.

2 cups warm water
1 package dry yeast
1/3 cup sugar
1 tablespoon salt
2 heaping tablespoons shortening
Flour

Mix 1 cup water with yeast and add sugar. Let stand for 5 minutes. Add 1 cup warm water, salt, and shortening. Add flour to make thick enough to knead. Knead for 10 minutes.

Place in covered bowl and let rise to double bulk. Punch down once after it starts to rise. Make into loaves or cinnamon rolls or buns.

Let rise again and bake at 350º until crust is brown and loaf sounds hollow when tapped.

Lee Whittlesey, Park Historian

"Mr. Yellowstone"—it's not an official title, but it sure fits. Few people in and around Yellowstone have not heard of Lee Whittlesey, park historian. Even fewer people—maybe none—have Lee's knowledge of the park.

As the country's first and oldest national park Yellowstone has incredible history, so it seems only logical that it have a historian. Lee says, "You can't run a park for the future if you don't know its past." In addition to Lee, Yellowstone also has archaeologists, anthropologists, cultural ethnologists, resource specialists, and architectural specialists.

Lee's interest in Yellowstone began as a young boy; he often vacationed here with his family. After college he held many Yellowstone jobs, from running a garbage truck to snow coach driver to law enforcement ranger, before becoming its historian. "I went to law school but decided I didn't want to spend all my time studying things that didn't interest me. What does interest me is the Greater Yellowstone area."

He can rattle off dates like phone numbers—"As a historian, dates are important"—but there is fieldwork, too. Lee and coworker Betsy Watry made a 16-mile round-trip hike in Hayden Valley to the Larry Matthews lunch station. Matthews, the first manager of Old Faithful Inn, ran several such stations in the late 1800s. Lee notes that there's an old stagecoach road that hasn't been used since the 1890s. "When you hike the road, it seems like you can hear the creaking of the wagon wheels."

Historians love to share their knowledge, and Lee's no exception, evident by the numerous books he's written. *Death in Yellowstone* is very popular, but his favorite is *A Guide to Yellowstone Waterfalls and Their Discovery*. "We discovered and added more than 300 waterfalls to the park maps." Unfortunately policy dictates that he can only propose names for the new falls, and they cannot be named after the discoverer.

"The military here kept very good records that resurfaced in the 1960s," he says. The park historian back then naively wrote to the national archives in Washington, D.C., asking for help with the records. Six months later the national archives police came to take them, but after years of meetings and arguments there was an agreement that Yellowstone would be a satellite facility—and remains the only park that is. "So we're allowed by special arrangement to keep our records."

The records are housed in grand style in the Yellowstone Heritage and Research Center, a modern building that's climate controlled and under heavy security, and where Lee spends most of his days. Located near the park's Gardiner entrance, the center is mainly for collections storage, although a rotating exhibit in the lobby is open to the public.

Yellowstone artifacts still turn up. "There's always someone who comes in with letters, ephemera, photos, arrowheads, and so on. And of course we search the Internet." The history here is bottomless, Lee notes, and with 30 years' worth of notes in his file drawers, he's not likely to run out of material anytime soon. In fact, it could translate into another book…if we're lucky.

Recipes by Lee Whittlesey

Pumpkin Bread

· · · · · · · · · · · · · · · · · · ·

Suzanne Lewis

This is the result of my fiddling with a recipe. I don't like pumpkin but I love pumpkin bread.

3 eggs
1$^1/_2$ cups sugar
1$^1/_2$ cups pumpkin
1 cup plus 2 tablespoons canola oil
1$^1/_2$ teaspoons vanilla
2$^1/_4$ cups flour
1$^1/_2$ teaspoons baking soda
1$^1/_2$ teaspoons baking powder
1$^1/_2$ teaspoons salt
1$^1/_2$ teaspoons cinnamon
$^1/_4$ teaspoon cloves
$^1/_4$ teaspoon ginger
$^1/_4$ teaspoon nutmeg
$^3/_4$ cup chopped pecans

Beat eggs and sugar together well. Add pumpkin, oil, and vanilla; mix thoroughly. Sift flour, soda, baking powder, salt, and spices. Add to pumpkin mixture, and beat. Add pecans. Bake at 350º for 1 hour in two well-greased loaf pans.

Sandwiches & Snacks

Norris Egg Salad Sandwiches

. . . .

Cheryl Jaworowski

When I work in Yellowstone's thermal areas, the smell of hydrogen sulfide gas makes me hungry for egg salad sandwiches. During the summer of 2003 I was working almost daily in Norris Geyser Basin. Because I made so many egg salad sandwiches that year, these sandwiches were named for the geyser basin.

Bread
2 hard-boiled eggs
2 tablespoons fat-free Miracle Whip
    dressing (or mayonnaise)
Chives (fresh or dried)
Crushed or chopped parsley (fresh or dried)
Paprika
Pinch of salt

Boil eggs, cool them and peel. Place eggs in a bowl and mix with dressing or mayo. Add chives, parsley, paprika, and salt. Mix well. Spread egg mixture on crusty sourdough bread or English muffins and enjoy.

Cheryl Jaworowski, Park Geologist

Some kids pile up pretty rocks under their beds that become forgotten collections tossed out by Mom on cleaning day. Cheryl Jaworowski's parents, however, allowed her to keep her little pieces of geology. The first in her family to go to college, Cheryl earned degrees in geology and taught herself astronomy, which resulted in her first job. It was on an airborne infrared observatory preparing star charts. As disparate as the two interests might seem, years later both would come into play at Yellowstone.

Cheryl's position as park geologist isn't limited to studying rocks. She's involved with interpretative rangers, archeologists, botanists, law enforcement (cases in which visitors take rocks or destroy thermal features), maintenance (road construction), and geothermal resources data. "We provide geological input for all of them."

She's often asked about Yellowstone's supervolcano that was portrayed by a BBC television program as impending gloom and doom. Cheryl isn't at all concerned. She says, "Yes, Yellowstone is an active volcano—we know that because of its earthquakes, the ground deformation, and the thermal features. The BBC talked to scientists to get an idea of what they think would happen, and although scientifically it's a good representation of a very, very unlikely event, the docudrama sensationalized it." (For more information check out the USGS website [http://volcanoes.usgs.gov/yvo], which has an excellent FAQ section.)

Today Cheryl is leading an impromptu tour around Mammoth Hot Springs, patiently explaining the geologic features. For example, regular park visitors might notice that the terraces seem to be drying up. But she explains that thermal waters are actually shifting as underground channels become plugged by minerals. "We want to protect the natural geologic process and find out what's happening. We hope to get thermal infrared information of major thermal areas once a year using airborne sensors," which is where Cheryl's alternate background comes in.

She points to Mount Everts, composed of Huckleberry Ridge Tuff from Yellowstone's first catastrophic eruption and from sediments 100 million years ago. Everts is a classic example of topographic inversion, meaning that what was once low topography is now high topography. Of the ridge's visible rock layers she says, "When those layers are thousands of feet underground and you cook them just right for the right amount of time, you get oil and gas if the rocks contain carbon, and these do."

The setting sun makes Bunsen Peak nearly glow. Cheryl says the mountain is a 50-million-year-old volcanic neck that wasn't covered by the last major catastrophic eruption of the Yellowstone volcano 640,000 years ago. The setting sun also concludes our tour. Cheryl adds, "I wouldn't want to be doing anything else—no matter where I go, I look at the landscape and speculate how it came to be. I count myself lucky to be working in a place like Yellowstone."

Cheri's Nut Mix

• • • • • • • • • • • • • • •

Cheryl Jaworowski

My favorite nut mix for hiking is a combination of other snacks and berries (see the recipe for Texas Pecans and Tamari Almonds).
Mix the pecans, almonds, pistachios, dried blueberries, cranberries, and cherries to your liking and enjoy along the trail.

Texas Pecans	Blueberries, dried
Tamari Almonds	Cranberries, dried
Pistachios	Cherries, dried

Recipes by Cheryl Jaworowski

Grilled Peanut Butter & Chocolate Chip Sandwich

Walter Voeller

This is ideal for grilling on a camping trip or as a cold and chunky sandwich on a day hike.
It packs easily and is a high-energy food.

Bread
Butter
Peanut butter
Chocolate chips

Put it all together and fry like a grilled cheese sandwich.

Walter Voeller, Fly-fishing Bellhop

 or years on vacations Walter Voeller slept in his Honda Civic wagon, ironic because he works for one of the most famous lodgings in the country: he's a bellhop at Old Faithful Inn. Working in the park allows Walter to pursue his real passion—fly fishing. So well known is his interest in backcountry trout that if you were to ask almost anyone at the inn for the bellhop fly-fishing bum, they'd know where to point.

Walter graduated from Sacramento State University in California with a major in social science/history. He held assorted jobs until he got hooked on fishing and as anyone who has picked up a travel brochure knows, Montana and Wyoming are a fly fisher's paradise. So Walter began a cycle of tying and selling his own flies, going to Yellowstone to fish, then tying and selling flies, until hiring on at the inn.

Walter says, "Bellhopping isn't a bad job—you don't make as much money as waiters but you can make a living at it." Toting bags keeps him stepping—with 327 rooms and 150 check-ins a night—but with many split shifts and good streams nearby, Walter can usually find time to fish around Old Faithful every day. On days off he'll hike into the backcountry—just far enough to get away from road noise and other anglers, set up his tent, and fish.

"I'm not sure exactly what the attraction is. I fish because it has a lot of variables—whole aspects of things to learn. No one can truly master everything about it—you try to get better at it. Mostly you're outside. The park encourages catch and release. You don't have to kill what you catch—a fish almost never swallows a fly, so it doesn't die from a hook in its throat."

Fish and bears go together but Walter's not too worried about bruins—he's more concerned about moose. "A moose was napping when I got to the stream. In the evening when the moose started to feed he kept staring at me and walking closer and closer and finally ran me out of the marsh." Walter shakes his head in disbelief as he recalls: "Once I saw a griz with a couple cubs and about 40 people actually chasing them. The mother bear started biting the lagging cub to speed it up. The bears were moving and the people jam was following it."

Walter's a shy person in a public job that's usually uneventful, but on occasion he rubs elbows with the famous: "I drove Ted Turner from the inn to Snow Lodge because it was raining; we talked a little fishing. I moved in Walter Cronkite's luggage (he had a handler like a rock star), and Michael J. Fox held the door open for me when I had a full cart of luggage."

Does anyone ever retire from bellhopping? Walter's not sure but admits he's getting older and is only a little concerned. "I'm kind of lazy about setting life goals, but if I'm happy being a bellhop I'm not going to worry about it."

Recipes by Walter Voeller

San-J Tamari Almonds

· · · · · · · · · · · · · · ·

Cheryl Jaworowski

Health food stores carry all the ingredients needed for Cheryl's almonds.

Organic almonds
San-J Tamari (wheat-free, reduced sodium,
    or regular)

Soak almonds in tamari (a kind of soy sauce). You can use wheat-free soy sauce, reduced-sodium soy sauce, or the naturally brewed tamari (premium soy sauce). Stir the almonds and tamari to evenly coat.

Place tamari-soaked almonds in a glass baking-dish and put them in a 350° oven. Bake for approximately 10 minutes or until almonds are lightly browned. Stir occasionally while baking.

Summer Delight Milkshakes

Dianna Kellie

This is very good with light strawberry/cinnamon flavoring.

Vanilla ice cream
Strawberry ice cream
Whipped topping
2% milk
Cinnamon

In blender, fill half full with vanilla ice cream. Add 1 scoop only of strawberry ice cream. Add $1/4$ cup whipped topping, cinnamon, and milk to cover ice cream; blend on high speed until creamy. Pour into two large glasses; top with whipped cream and serve.

Texas Pecans

· · · · · · · · · · · · · · · · · · ·

Cheryl Jaworowski

Friends living in Florida and Wyoming introduced me to these wonderful snacks and garnishes for salads and desserts. I make the following version and enjoy eating them on fresh garden salads with sliced avocado wedges or on top of steamed cinnamon apples. The best ingredients make the best tasting Texas Pecans, so buy the plumpest pecans you can.

Plump pecans

Coating:
1 to 2 cups of fructose
2 to 4 tablespoons paprika
$1/4$ teaspoon chipotle chili powder
$1/4$ teaspoon cumin (optional)

Mix a cup or two of fructose with paprika and chipotle powder. Add more chipotle powder or º teaspoon of cayenne powder if you prefer more of a kick. Stir dry ingredients until thoroughly mixed. This mixture makes several batches and stays fresh when kept in a sealed glass jar.

Preheat oven to 350º. Place pecans in a glass baking dish. Sprinkle 2 tablespoons of spice mixture over the nuts, and bake. When fructose spice mixture is melted over the pecans (5 or 10 minutes), stir with a fork to evenly coat. You may wish to add another tablespoon of the fructose spice mixture over the pecans. Bake for another 5 to 10 minutes or until the fructose spice glaze is slightly browned. Let cool on a wire rack, stirring occasionally with a fork.

Note: Fructose browns easily. It is a natural sugar found in fruit that is metabolized more slowly than refined sugar.

Wild Alaska Salmon BLT

. . . .

OLD FAITHFUL SNOW LODGE
Chef Jim Chapman

8 slices nine-grain bread
12 slices tomato
12 slices cooked bacon

4 leaves Romaine lettuce
1/4 cup wasabi mayonnaise
   (for wasabi mayonnaise, add wasabi
   powder to mayonnaise until desired
   strength is reached)
1/2 pound cold smoked wild Alaska salmon

Toast bread and spread with wasabi mayonnaise. Place one leaf of romaine, three slices of tomato, and bacon on each sandwich. Place 2 ounces of smoked salmon on each sandwich; close and cut in half corner-to-corner.

Yield 4 sandwiches

Appetizers

Bacon-Wrapped Water Chestnuts

· · · · · · · · · · · ·

Sue & Jack Davis

1 to 3 cans water chestnuts
   (depending on how many appetizers needed)
1 pound thick bacon; cut slices in half
1 cup ketchup
2 tablespoons brown sugar

Wrap half a piece of bacon around a water chestnut (it should go around about $1^1/_2$ times) and secure loose end with a wooden toothpick. Place upright on a broiler pan. Heat oven to 400º and cook appetizers until bacon is crisp.

Mix together ketchup and brown sugar and serve in a small bowl for dipping sauce.

Recipes by Sue and Jack Davis

Sue & Jack Davis, Memorable Memorabilia

In 1967 Sue Davis dropped a gallon of chocolate syrup on the floor of the West Yellowstone Dairy Queen where she worked between high school and college. Her cooking skills have improved considerably since then. In fact, husband Jack claims it wasn't only Sue's charms that wowed him. "It was a matter of survival. I was living alone and not much of a cook and Sue makes the most incredible corn chowder, so it seemed only natural we get married," he jokes.

Although Sue is an amazing cook, food took a backseat to a more lucrative passion. During her DQ days she started collecting Yellowstone park ephemera, beginning with a postcard. "Then people started giving me items, and I began collecting everything." Ten years later Jack came along, and soon both were avidly seeking park memorabilia.

The collecting bug bit Jack hard. One time on a fishing trip when he had left his wallet behind, he had to beg money from his fishing buddies to buy a Limoges Old Faithful plate in an antique shop. "They thought I was nuts when I asked them to fork over their beer money for a plate, but they agreed. I got my plate and there was money left for beer—we all went home happy."

Sue and Jack's collection grew to 10,000 postcards and another 10,000 miscellaneous items that included an old ranger uniform, an Old Faithful Inn key fob, brochures, photographs, dolls, and others. The rarest are coated specimens, which Sue explains are turn-of-the-century objects tourists dropped off at the Mammoth Hot Springs coating terrace. "The piece would be soaked in the hot springs and coated with minerals by the end of the day, and the tourist would take the souvenir home, but few of these survived."

They collected…and collected. "We didn't pass on anything—our house became a storage facility," says Jack, noting it was a challenge to find space for a ten-by-five-foot road sign, complete with bullet holes. Sue adds, "We collected when Yellowstone memorabilia wasn't popular, but it's now the most collectible park in the world, whether because of Old Faithful or its being the first park or because we drove the interest," she laughs, "we're not sure."

Word got out about the Davises. They were featured on television where Sue said they made an impression, mostly before the show. "Ten minutes before going live, I dropped my mike in the toilet and it was a mad dash to dry it off." Fortunately other events have been less chaotic, such as the opening of the Yellowstone Historic Center in West Yellowstone where their treasures were on loan.

They decided to clean house. "We cataloged 3,000 items but that took two years and we realized we wouldn't live long enough to finish," so they donated and sold off part of the collection, all of which is housed in the Yellowstone Heritage and Research Center in Gardiner.

Through collecting comes knowledge. Even today the park calls the Davises for information. And it's rare if they don't have the answer—about as rare as a mineral-coated souvenir.

Cheesy Treat

Ruth & Leslie Quinn

10 ounces Velveeta cheese
$1/2$ pound cooked pork sausage
2 16-ounce jars of chunky salsa
(mild or medium to taste)

Cut Velveeta into 2-inch blocks. Place into large microwave-safe bowl. Pour salsa and sausage on top of cheese. Microwave on high for about 5 minutes, stopping to stir several times until the cheese is melted and the mixture is warm. Serve warm with corn chips.

Cowboy Chip Dip

Barbara Forbes Rinker
We always take this to our Wyoming get-togethers and BBQs. It's always a hit.

Layer:
1 16-ounce can Hormel Chili without beans
1 8-ounce package softened Philadelphia cream cheese
1 can diced green chilies
1 can of chopped olives

Add generous amount of grated cheddar cheese on top.

Bake 350º for 15 minutes.

Serve with tortilla chips.

Creamy Chicken Spread

. . . .

Carolyn Wallen

1 package (8 ounces) cream cheese, softened
1/2 cup sour cream
1 teaspoon dried minced onion
1/2 teaspoon onion salt
1/2 teaspoon Worcestershire sauce
1/4 teaspoon cayenne pepper
2 cans (10 ounces) chunk white chicken, drained
Paprika, optional

In a mixing bowl, combine the first six ingredients. Fold in chicken.

Cover and refrigerate for at least 1 hour.

Sprinkle with paprika if desired. Serve with crackers.

Makes about 3 cups

Hot Brie Appetizer

. . . .

Tom & Bonnie Murphy
To give this a slightly different flavor, brown the pecans in a little oil first.

8-inch round of brie

Mix together:
3 tablespoons chopped pecans
3 tablespoons brown sugar
Brandy to moisten

In a 425° oven, bake brie in an ovenproof dish for 5 to 6 minutes. Top brie with brandy pecan mixture. Bake at 350° for another 5 minutes or until center is soft.

Serve on hot dish with crackers.

Red Bell Pepper Hummus

Cheryl Jaworowski

Usually I use canned, cooked organic garbanzo beans, but you can also buy chickpeas and cook them yourself. Red bell pepper hummus makes a quick, easy, and tasty alternative sandwich.

1 can cooked garbanzo beans (chickpeas)
1/2 diced red bell pepper
1/4 cup tahini
Juice of 1 fresh lemon
3 to 5 cloves of fresh garlic
Parsley (fresh or dried)
Chives (fresh or dried)
1/2 cup water
Salt to taste

Drain water from garbanzo beans. Blend cooked beans, bell pepper, tahini, lemon juice, garlic, parsley, chives, water, and salt in a blender. Mixture should be a thick paste. Add more tahini if you need to thicken the mixture or more water to thin.

Spread the mixture on a toasted bagel with lettuce for a sandwich that packs well, or eat with wedges of pita and a fresh garden salad.

Shrimp Toast

· · · · · · · · · · · · · · · · · · ·

Suzanne Lewis
This reminds me of when my husband and I lived on the Gulf Coast.
We met during my first assignment as a park ranger at Gulf Islands National Seashore.

8 very thin white sandwich bread slices
1 pound peeled medium shrimp
1 medium onion, chopped
1-inch piece of fresh ginger, peeled
   and chopped
1/2 teaspoon salt
1/2 teaspoon pepper
2 egg whites
1/2 cup bread crumbs
Vegetable oil
Garnish with lemon slices

Trim crust from bread, and cut each slice into 4 triangles. Set aside.

Peel shrimp and devein. Process shrimp and next four ingredients in a blender or food processor until smooth, scraping down sides. With blender or processor running, add egg whites and process till blended.

Spread mixture over each bread triangle. Coat with bread crumbs and chill 1 hour. Pour oil to 2 inches in a heavy skillet. Fry in batches, 3 minutes on each side or until golden brown. Drain on paper towels.

Makes 32 triangles

Suzanne Lewis, *Park Superintendent*

S uzanne Lewis loves to cook, that is, when she's not managing a 2.2-million acre national park, overseeing 400-plus employees, and dealing with the more than three million tourists who visit Yellowstone National Park annually. In 2002 she took on the job of park superintendent, the first woman to hold the position.

She says, "I have a wonderful job, but it's hard work communicating across all the boundaries in and outside the park. I don't think I'll ever be as challenged as I am here, and I like a challenge." She adds there's no greater job than to work for the National Park Service, and many would agree there's no better place to do it than Yellowstone.

It takes a lot to make the park run, and Suzanne chuckles at what constitutes a typical day: "With that many people, natural features, and wildlife, there is no 'typical,' although wildlife jams are common. When 2,000 bison decide to cross the road in Hayden, you can be

there for a while." But for every hassle she says you don't have to look far to find a blessing, and Suzanne finds it in the visitors. "They're so excited to be here. Most have never been in the park before, have never seen wildlife in its native habitat, and are visiting an ecosystem for the first time in their lives."

It doesn't take a first-timer to be in awe of the park's attractions. Suzanne thinks only a split second before recalling the most exciting thing she's experienced in Yellowstone. "Steamboat Geyser—the world's tallest—has gone off three times. It has no schedule and had not erupted in nine years before I got here, then it erupted three times in four years. I saw it twice."

She credits her parents for her interest in the outdoors and a college roommate's father, who was a park ranger, for encouraging her to become a ranger. She began college on a premed track then decided she liked history better and changed her major. That history, interestingly, carries over to her cooking. "I have two very old recipe books—one spiral-bound, food all over it, falling apart, taped together, and a 1920s hardbound cookbook passed down from my grandmother to my mother to me."

All her recipes have a history or story connected to them. Her shrimp toast reminds her of her first assignment as a park ranger at Gulf Islands National Seashore, where she met her husband. Her carrot cake is her grandmother's recipe. "My mother made this cake every year for my husband and as she aged she'd occasionally forget the carrots, but it's still a good cake without them. The Brunswick stew is from my husband's Aunt Olene—he has fond memories of eating it in Alabama."

As park spokesperson Suzanne often is on the road during the year, whether locally, in Washington, D.C., or internationally. During precious free time at home in Mammoth Hot Springs, she likes to relax with a good recipe, but Suzanne does more than just cook—she makes history.

Recipes by Suzanne Lewis

Spinach Dip with Round Bread

Barbara Forbes Rinker

My sister-in-law, Dayle Rinker, made this for our Rinker reunion held here in Wyoming.

1 carton soft cream cheese
1 carton sour cream
1 package Hidden Valley Buttermilk
   Ranch dressing, dry
1 package chopped frozen spinach, thawed

Mix together the cream cheese, sour cream, and ranch dressing. Add the spinach.

Cut the center from a loaf of round bread, and put dip in loaf. Use the cut-out center (cubed) or vegetables for dipping.

Stuffed Mushrooms Gazpacho Style

Jack & Tina Gilchrist

½ pound medium mushrooms
½ cup finely diced tomatoes
2 tablespoons minced celery
2 tablespoons finely chopped cucumber
1 tablespoon each minced radish,
   green pepper, onion
⅛ teaspoon garlic powder
12 tablespoons Italian salad dressing
Freshly ground black pepper to taste

Rinse, pat dry, and remove stems from mushrooms. Combine remaining ingredients and mix well.

Spoon mixture into mushroom caps. Chill until ready to serve.

Jack Gilchrist, Bear Watcher

If you see a horde of cars clogging a park road, you might find Jack Gilchrist there, but he won't be directing traffic. This is a bear jam, and Jack watches bears. Of course few bruins sit along the road, so Jack says that you need a spotting scope or good binoculars, and you need to know where to look. Since retiring as a sociology professor from Montana State University, Jack has more time to spend locating and observing bears.

To find grizzlies, Jack suggests the Lamar Valley between the picnic area and Pebble Creek. For black bears he says, "It's difficult to get from Tower Junction to Tower Falls and not run into one or two jams." You can find bears any time of day but the best chance for checking one off of your to-do list is early morning and dusk. Jack should know: in one 24-hour period he saw 22 bears, 16 of them grizzlies.

Normally he goes by himself or with his wife, Tina, but once inside the park he meets up with a small gang of regular bear watchers. "One of the most rewarding aspects of watching is sharing our findings with first-time sighters," he says. A bad bear day? It's a rare day when a bear isn't spotted, but when it does happen, mountain goats, wolves, and birds are Jack's focus. His observations eventually turned into a broadened knowledge of bear behavior, such as:

- The courting period is May and June for blacks and grizzlies. Normally the male follows the female; she tries to evade but he stays within about 50 yards. "I once saw five pairs of courting griz in three hours."
- Cubs do play. If there's still snow on the ground, they slide down hills on their butts while the mother grubs for food.
- Interaction: "A sow with two cubs was on a carcass. Six wolves approached, circled her, doing all they could to get to the carcass. The cubs sat on her back while she held off the wolves."
- An intimidating name means nothing. In Lamar a big black bear chased a grizzly that wanted nothing to do with the black bear.

Jack warns: "Never approach any bear—it's unlikely you'll outrun it." He tells of an elderly woman who, along with a group of people, was watching a grizzly on a far riverbank. The bear crossed the river and chased everyone to their vehicles, but no one would let the woman in their car. She finally managed to get to her car, jump in, and close the door just as the bear reached her. She was unusually fortunate.

He also says there are good reasons for the signs that ban wildlife feeding. One time someone left a "bad" camp in the backcountry and a beautiful grizzly found food there. Then the bear began going after tents in campgrounds. It had to be trapped and euthanized.

Some of what Jack knows about bears was learned at the Yellowstone Institute, where he's helped out as a wildlife spotter. If you're lucky enough to meet Jack on one of his park outings, stop and ask about bears. He'll gladly show you the one focused in his spotting scope.

Recipes by Jack Gilchrist

Boiling River Divinity ... 141
Lamb Meatballs ... 104
Mrs. Burns's Lemon Pie ... 154
Pork'n Apples with Rice ... 120
Stuffed Mushrooms Gazpacho Style... 52

Stuffed Mushrooms

Joe Bueter

20 fresh mushrooms
2 tablespoons butter, melted
1/4 cup butter, melted
3 tablespoons green onion, chopped
1 tablespoon flour
1/4 cup milk
1 clove garlic, pressed
3 tablespoons parsley, chopped
3 tablespoons feta cheese, crumbled
1/4 cup Parmesan cheese, shredded
Salt and pepper to taste

Clean mushrooms; remove and save stems. Brush mushroom caps with 2 tablespoons melted butter. Sauté chopped mushroom stems and onions in 1/4 cup butter until dry. Add flour and mix well. Add milk, garlic, parsley, feta, and mix together.

Stuff mushroom caps with this mixture. Sprinkle with Parmesan cheese. Bake in hot oven (400° at least) a few minutes.

Sweet & Sour Beef Meatballs

. . . .

MAMMOTH HOT SPRINGS HOTEL
Chef Jim Chapman

2 slices white bread
1 egg
1 pound ground beef
1/4 cup minced onion
1/4 cup beef broth
1/2 teaspoon minced garlic
1/2 teaspoon salt
1/2 teaspoon paprika
1/4 teaspoon black pepper
Pinch dry thyme
1/2 pound plum tomatoes, canned and peeled
1/4 cup brown sugar
1/4 cup sugar
1/4 cup gingersnaps, crumbled
4 tablespoons lemon juice

Preheat oven to 350º.

Dip bread in cold water until saturated; drain, squeeze out excess water.

Combine egg, beef, onion, broth, garlic, salt, paprika, pepper, and thyme. Shape into balls and bake until done (155º internal temperature).

Drain tomatoes; heat with sugars, gingersnaps, and lemon juice until the sugar dissolves, then puree. Add meatballs and simmer until glazed. Sauce can be thickened with a little cornstarch if necessary.

Yield 25 meatballs

Texas Caviar

Carolyn Wallen

Serve this dip warm with chips and crackers.

15-ounce can black-eyed peas with jalapeño, drained and mashed
4-ounce can chopped green chilies
2 tablespoons butter
2 tablespoons finely chopped green onion
$1/8$ teaspoon garlic powder
5-ounce jar Old English sharp cheese spread

Combine all ingredients in microwavable dish and microwave for 3 to 4 minutes, stirring often, until cheese is melted and dip is hot.

Wild Alaska Salmon Firecracker Rolls with Sweet Hot Chili Sauce

. . . .

MAMMOTH HOT SPRINGS HOTEL
Chef Jim Chapman

1/2 pound wild Alaska salmon, raw
1 teaspoon Tabasco
1/4 teaspoon salt
28 wonton wrappers
1 ounce baby spinach
Water as needed
1/4 cup honey
1/4 cup hot chili sauce
1 pint peanut oil

Pass salmon through meat grinder and mix with Tabasco and salt.

Lay out wonton wrappers with a spinach leaf in the center. The spinach leaf should be smaller than the wonton wrapper. Place one teaspoon of salmon mixture on the bottom center of wonton wrapper. Wet sides and top edge of wrapper with water. Fold sides of wrapper in 1/2 inch and roll salmon inside wrapper from bottom to top.

Heat oil to 350° in frying pan. Cook firecracker rolls until golden brown, turning over to evenly brown.

For dipping sauce combine honey with hot chili sauce.

Yield 4 portions

Soups

Cabbage Soup

· · · · · · · · · · · · · · · · · ·

Cheryl Jaworowski

This easy vegetable soup is a reminder of harvest time, friends, cool weather, my father-in-law, and simple northern European traditions. This can be a very colorful soup when made with various potatoes: red, true blue, fingerlings, or Yukon Gold.

Blue potatoes
Yukon Gold or fingerling potatoes
5 carrots
1/2 head green cabbage
5 stalks celery
3 green onions
5 cloves of garlic
Parsley (fresh or dried)
Water or soup stock

Optional: For a spicy (volcanic) version of this soup, add a dash of cayenne.

Wash vegetables. Cut blue potatoes into circles, Yukon Gold potatoes into cubes, carrots into circles or cubes, and cabbage into strips. Place into slow cooker with celery, onions, garlic, and parsley. Cover vegetables with water or a stock and heat on a stovetop or in slow cooker (about 4 hours) until vegetables are tender.

Serve with crackers or flatbread and cheese as a side dish.

Chicken Wild Rice Soup

Carolyn Wallen

5 2/3 cups water
1 package (4.3 ounces) long grain and
  wild rice mix
1 envelope chicken noodle soup mix
1 celery rib, chopped
1 medium carrot, chopped
1/3 cup onion, chopped
2 cans (10 3/4-ounce cans) condensed
  cream of chicken soup, undiluted
1 cup cooked chicken, cubed

In a large saucepan, combine water, rice with contents of seasoning packet, and soup mix. Bring to a boil. Reduce heat, cover, and simmer for 10 minutes.

Stir in celery, carrot, and onion. Cover and simmer for 10 minutes. Stir in chicken soup and chicken. Cook 8 minutes longer or until vegetables are tender.

Egg Drop Soup

Cheryl Jaworowski

Egg drop soup is easy to make and the variations are endless. The healthful balance of herbs and the elegance of this soup reminds me of an Asian-American friend.

Grated fresh ginger, to taste
5 cloves fresh garlic
3 green onions
2 tablespoons sesame oil
1 cup potato soup stock or vegetable
   or chicken broth
3 leaves red Swiss chard
3 stalks celery, chopped
Parsley, to taste
1 tablespoon tamari
Water
1 egg, beaten

In a saucepan, sauté grated ginger, garlic, and onions in sesame oil on medium heat. Add 1 cup potato soup stock, chard, celery, parsley, tamari, and water. Bring water and vegetables to a boil. When water is boiling, drop in beaten egg. Turn down heat to low and simmer for a few minutes.

Variations: Add firm tofu, chicken, or shrimp. Replace Swiss chard with spinach, peas, or corn. For a spicy (volcanic) version of this soup, add a dash of cayenne.

Homemade Turkey Soup

Dianna Kellie

This is a good way to use that seasoned turkey carcass left over from Thanksgiving or Christmas.

1 turkey carcass
1 can peas
1 can corn
Garden carrots
1 can green beans
1 can crushed tomatoes
1 can whole potatoes
1/8 cup all-season salt

In a large stockpot half filled with water, add carcass and boil until remaining meat flakes off. This could take an hour or so depending on the size of the bird and how much meat is on the bones.

Take carcass out of pot and remove remaining meat. Add meat back to pot; discard bones. Add peas, corn, carrots, green beans, tomatoes, and potatoes to pot. Season to taste. Simmer for 45 minutes more.

Serves 6

Lentil Soup

. . . .

Doug Smith

Lentils are a great source of protein and convenient for backpacking. This soup goes well with wild game as well as beef. There are no amounts for the ingredients—add as much or little as you want.

1/2 bag lentils, soaked 4 to 6 hours
Raw carrots
Raw onions
Canned whole tomatoes
Ground beef/deer/elk, browned
Parsley, salt, and pepper

Boil lentils 30 minutes. Add carrots, onions, and tomatoes, cook 1 hour. Add browned meat, parsley, salt, and pepper.

Doug Smith, Wolf Leader

Doug Smith's phone rings every few minutes. Today he's fielding a call from a Norwegian visitor who's going to be in the park only for a few days and wants to see wolves. Other calls involve straightening out an invoice and making arrangements for a small plane for an aerial elk count, depending on the weather. "We do most of our work from aircraft," says Doug, Yellowstone National Park's wolf project leader.

Little in the park's recent history has sparked as much controversy as the 1995-96 reintroduction of *Canis lupus.* Doug still takes flak about them: "Any wolf is too many wolves for some people."

So why were wolves reintroduced? As ordered, park personnel killed the last one in 1926, but the Endangered Species Act, passed almost 50 years later, mandated that endangered animals be restored to appropriate habitat. After about 20 more years of discussion and exhaustive paperwork, wild wolves were released in Yellowstone.

Many ranchers complain, yet statistics confirm that the number one killer of livestock is dogs—wolves are way down on the list. "Only 0.0001 percent of livestock that die in Montana are due to wolves—it's minuscule," Doug says.

Although not winning over any converts, Doug says, "We've gained ranchers' respect because we've kept our promise—if any livestock is killed, the wolf is killed, and that's happened in every case." Interactions with livestock are not as common as he predicted. What no one could forecast, however, was their effect on the ecosystem—coyotes, bears, and elk have felt the wolves' presence. Even the vegetation (as a result of changes in elk behavior) isn't immune to change, "but it's a positive effect—it creates more diversity."

Along with bears and Old Faithful, wolves have become one of the main reasons people visit Yellowstone. It was estimated that wolf watching would generate $23 million annually for the park and surrounding towns, but actual revenue is closer to $35 million and climbing. Doug says, "There can be 200 to 300 people waiting for a wolf to show in the Lamar Valley—it's that big a deal."

Doug's interest in wild canines began as a young boy and continued through college—the first jobs he had after graduation were with wolves. He studied them in Minnesota and Michigan for 13 years and considers himself fortunate to have this job. "It's what I've always wanted. Sometimes my wife gives me a hard time because I can't wait for the weekend to end to get back to work."

Unfortunately, Doug spends less time in the field—his job now more administrative than hands-on. "There's pressure to be in the office all the time, but I feel you can't study wolves from behind a desk. You need to be out there with them, at least sometimes."

Recipes by Doug Smith

Sausage Onion Soup

· · · · · · · · · · · · · · · · ·

Tom & Bonnie Murphy
This comes from the Uptown Café in Butte, Montana.

1 pound Italian sausage (hot or sweet or
    mix of both), cut into 1-inch pieces
2 tablespoons olive oil
1 large Spanish onion (about 12 ounces),
    coarsely chopped
2 teaspoons minced garlic
1/4 cup firmly packed light brown sugar
1/2 cup dry white wine
2 tablespoons Dijon mustard
8 cups beef broth
2 tablespoons minced fresh flatleaf parsley,
    plus additional for garnish

In a heavy kettle, sauté sausage in oil over moderately high heat, stirring, until browned, about 3 minutes. Pour off fat and add onion and garlic. Cook 3 to 5 minutes or until onion is soft. Add remaining ingredients and simmer with lid ajar about 1 hour. Add salt and pepper to taste. Serve garnished with parsley.

Makes about 10 cups

Sue's Corn Chowder

· · · · · · · · · · · · · · · · · ·

Sue & Jack Davis

Jack notes that this soup goes especially well with a Green Bay Packers game.

1 to 1½ pounds bacon
2½ to 3 onions
About 5 pounds potatoes
3 cans creamed corn (14¾-ounce can)
3 to 4 cups milk (depending on how
   thick you want the chowder)

Cut bacon into 1-inch pieces and fry until crisp. Save the fat. Chop the onions and sauté in the bacon fat until tender; drain and set aside. Peel the potatoes and cut into bite-sized pieces; boil until not quite soft, and drain.

In a large heavy kettle combine the creamed corn and milk, then add the bacon, onions, and potatoes. Simmer on low for about 30 minutes.

This makes between 1 and 2 gallons; freeze the extra or invite the gang over for soup, bread, and football.

Sweet Corn Bisque
with Linguica Sausage & Pumpkin Seeds

LAKE HOTEL
Chef Jim Chapman

1/4 cup butter
1 onion, diced
1/4 cup all purpose flour
3 pounds whole kernel corn
1 potato, peeled and diced
1 1/2 quarts vegetable stock
1 pint heavy cream
1/2 teaspoon turmeric
Salt and white pepper to taste
5 ounces linguica sausage cut into
    thin half moons
1/4 cup pumpkin seeds

Melt butter and sauté onions until translucent. Add flour and make roux. Add remaining ingredients except linguica and pumpkin seeds. Bring to boil while whisking occasionally. Lower to simmer and cook until potatoes are very soft. Puree soup, and strain. Adjust seasoning and consistency. Finish with 1/2 ounce linguica sausage and sprinkle of pumpkin seeds.

Yield 10 portions

Tomato Spinach Lentil Soup

Cheryl Jaworowski

Plump, juicy tomatoes from the garden are a wonderful base for a tasty vegetarian soup.
During late summer I gather tomatoes from my garden, wash them, cut off the tops,
stick them in a blender, and freeze the puree, which provides the base for many winter soups.
This soup was inspired by a visit to Minneapolis and a wonderful Greek restaurant.

1 cup lentils
1 to 2 cups tomato puree
Chopped spinach
At least 5 cloves of garlic
Paprika
Cumin powder or seeds
Parsley (fresh or dried)
Basil (fresh or dried)
1 bunch green onions, sliced
1 tablespoon olive oil
Salt to taste
Water or soup stock

Optional: For a spicy (volcanic) version of this soup, add a dash of **cayenne**.

Cook lentils until soft. Combine lentils, tomato puree, spinach, garlic, paprika, cumin, parsley, basil, green onions, olive oil, and salt in a pot or slow cooker; add water until soup is an appropriate consistency. On a stovetop, cook for 20 to 30 minutes on medium heat; in a slow cooker, 4 hours.

Serve with crackers or flatbread and cheese as a side dish. Steamed cinnamon apples top off this tasty fall supper for dessert.

Tuscan Bean Soup

MAMMOTH HOT SPRINGS HOTEL
Chef Jim Chapman

1/2 ounce vegetable oil
8 ounces diced onions
4 ounces diced celery
4 ounces diced carrot
1/2 tablespoon minced garlic
1 teaspoon chopped fresh rosemary
1/2 tablespoon fresh thyme
1 1/2 quarts chicken stock
1 1/2 cups tomato juice
1 1/2 cups diced tomatoes
1 1/2 cups cooked cannelloni beans
   (or other white beans)
2 ounces fresh spinach, chopped
1/4 cup chopped parsley
1/4 cup chopped fresh basil
Salt and pepper to taste
2 tablespoons cornstarch to adjust consistency

Heat oil in pot; sauté onions, celery, carrots, and garlic until tender, about 5 minutes. Add rosemary, thyme, chicken stock, tomato juice, diced tomatoes, and beans. Bring to boil, then down to simmer. Cook 30 minutes. Add spinach, parsley, and basil.

Mix cornstarch with a little water to make a slurry. Slowly add to simmering soup while stirring until desired consistency. Taste and add salt and pepper as necessary.

Yield 10 portions

Salads

Anything Goes Fresh Vegetable Salad

Sue & Jack Davis

This is a make as you go, anything goes salad. Use as much or as little as you like of each of the following:

Cucumbers, peeled and sliced
Zucchini (don't peel but remove soft centers)
Cherry tomatoes
Cauliflower
Celery
Radishes
Broccoli
Green onions, 1 bunch
$1/2$ can ripe olives
1 8-ounce bottle Italian dressing
    with 2 tablespoons sugar added to bottle

Into a large bowl, cut up vegetables into bite-sized pieces. Pour dressing over veggies and marinate in refrigerator for 5 to 6 hours, stirring occasionally.

Aunt Blanche's Cranberry Salad

. . . .

Barbara Forbes Rinker

*This is from my husband's Aunt Blanche Martz. She always made this for
Thanksgiving dinner when we went to the family farm in southern Illinois.*

2 cups fresh cranberries
1 cup sugar
1 cup seedless grapes
1/4 cup nuts (pecans or walnuts)
1/2 pint whipped cream or Cool Whip.

Grind cranberries with meat grinder; add sugar. Let drain overnight. Halve the grapes; add them and nuts to drained cranberries. Put into whipped cream.

Broccoli Salad

. . . .

Bob Richard

Salad:

   2 large bunches broccoli, flowerets only
   $1/2$ to $3/4$ cup bacon, cooked and crumbled
   $1/2$ pound mushrooms, sliced
   4 ounces sunflower seeds, toasted
   1 large red onion, sliced in rings

Combine broccoli, bacon, mushrooms, sunflower seeds, and onion.

Dressing:

   1 cup mayonnaise
   $1/2$ cup sugar
   4 tablespoons red wine vinegar

Blend the mayonnaise, sugar, and vinegar and refrigerate several hours or overnight.

Pour dressing over salad just before serving and toss to coat.

Creole Potato Salad

· · · · · · · · · · · · · · · · · ·

Suzanne Lewis

My husband doesn't like mayonnaise, and because it's difficult to make potato salad for one person, I created this recipe using only a scant amount of mayo to disguise its presence.

3 pounds red potatoes, cubed
1/2 cup mayonnaise
1/2 cup Creole mustard
1 tablespoon red wine vinegar
1 teaspoon salt
1 teaspoon prepared horseradish
1/2 teaspoon dried thyme
1/4 teaspoon garlic powder
1/4 teaspoon ground red pepper
6 hard-cooked eggs, chopped
1 medium sweet onion, diced

Cook potatoes in boiling salted water to cover for about 12 minutes, until tender; drain and cool slightly. Stir together mayonnaise, Creole mustard, plus next six ingredients in large bowl; add potatoes, eggs, and onion, and toss gently. Serve at room temperature or chilled.

Family Favorite Potato Salad

· · · · · · · · · · · · · · · · · ·

Dianna Kellie

This is a 2-day project, but the results are worth it!

8 large potatoes (russets work well)
1 dozen eggs
1 bunch green onions
6 stalks celery
6 dill pickles, cubed
1 small brick colby cheese
2 cups mayonnaise
1 teaspoon mustard
1/8 cup dill pickle juice
Parsley
Paprika

The night before, boil potatoes in one pot; when fork inserted comes out easily, they're done. Hard boil eggs in another pan. Cool both to room temperature, then refrigerate overnight. While eggs and potatoes are cooking, slice green onions in small pieces, place in airtight container and refrigerate. Cube the celery in small pieces, then place in its own container. Do the same for the pickles and cheese, about 1/4-inch cubes; place each in own container and refrigerate.

Next day, peel and cube potatoes and place in a large bowl. Shell and cube hard-boiled eggs and add to potatoes. Add onions, celery, pickles, and cheese. In a separate bowl, mix mayonnaise, mustard, and pickle juice to taste. You may add more of these ingredients if you want more sauce. Add sauce to potato salad and mix gently. Add paprika and parsley sprigs and it's ready to serve.

Grizzly Camp Salad: 24-Hour Cabbage Salad

Bob Richard

1 head shredded cabbage
1 large onion, chopped
3/4 cup sugar
3/4 cup vinegar
1 tablespoon prepared mustard
1 teaspoon salt
1 teaspoon celery seed
2 teaspoons mustard seed
3/4 cup oil

Layer cabbage and onion in bowl; sprinkle with sugar. Bring to boil vinegar, prepared mustard, salt, celery seed, and mustard seed. Remove from heat and add oil. Cool.

Pour over cabbage, refrigerate overnight. Store in refrigerator.

Bob Richard, Grub Steak Tours

There are tours of Yellowstone and its surroundings and then there are great tours. Bob Richard's Grub Steak Expeditions falls under the second heading. Young, old, special needs, politicians, celebrities, pipe fitters, Elderhostels—Bob accommodates everyone. Like everything he does, it's top quality and it's *all* through word of mouth.

Bob's a third-generation entrepreneur: his grandfather began offering Yellowstone tours in 1906, escorting guests of Buffalo Bill Cody; his father was licensed as a park photographer. Bob got *his* Yellowstone knowledge as a park ranger (he was the park's last appointed horse ranger) and became licensed to guide tours in photography, history, fishing, hiking, and transportation, all of which more than qualify him to serve 1,400 to 1,900 customers a year. Of course, he can't do it alone, which is why he finds the best people in their fields to lead his trips. "I have 17 guides who specialize in geology, forests, wolves, bears, fly fishing—we make it fit the occasion and the customer," Bob says.

Don't expect to call Bob the night before you want to see a wolf in the park. His trips are booked two years in advance. "I don't do spur-of-the-moment tours," he says. People tell him what they want and he'll do it, always with the utmost safety of the customer in mind. A bull elk can punch holes in the side of a car—he's seen it happen. "Even though I carry insurance, I never want to have to fill out an accident report—never had to either." He's also never had a complaint.

His customers, many of them repeats, want a hassle-free vacation that provides them the most of what they want for the time spent. Wolves and bears are the most requested, but Bob often scouts in advance for specific, unusual wildlife, flowers, or the perfect trout hangout. "I once had a family by the name of Wolf, and we spent three days finding wolves for their daughter."

Guests eat on the fly. "We provide a field lunch because we don't want to spend a lot of time sitting in a restaurant when we could be out seeing and learning." He gets his rave bandana lunches from a cafe in Cody, but he is an accomplished cook. "I can make antelope taste like the best beef you're ever had." Many people have encouraged

Bob to publish a cookbook—an idea he's entertained—but it may have to wait. Besides leading and organizing tours, Bob manages his company's website and oversees a Yellowstone CD plus his book, *Yellowstone Country*, a fascinating introduction to his father's 60 years of black-and-white photography.

For visitors coming to the region for the first time and who don't know exactly what they want, wwwgrubsteaktours.com offers tour suggestions. Bob notes he's fully aware of the misspelling. "I wanted a catchy name for the business. Someone lent me money to get started—that's a grubstake—but this spelling is more memorable."

If you want more than a tour—perhaps an experience of a lifetime—Bob Richard will see that you get it. The grub isn't bad either.

Recipes by Bob Richard

Bob's Ranch Biscuits ... 25
Broccoli Salad ... 75
Grizzly Camp Salad: 24-Hour Cabbage Salad ... 78
Hollandaise Sauce ... 173
Macaroni and Cheese Soufflé ... 106
Oven Roast Potatoes ... 134
Pass Creek Pasta ... 134
Pecan Chicken ... 118
Phonograph's Sourdough Sponge and Hotcakes ... 14
Rhea's Meatloaf ... 121
Sunlight Lemon Pie ... 167
Whistle Creek Almond Roca ... 169

No Bones Hot Chicken Salad

Joe Bueter

1¹/₂ to 2 pounds, chicken, cooked
   (2 cups diced)
2 cups celery, diced fine
¹/₂ cups almonds, sliced
2 tablespoons onion, chopped
2 tablespoons lemon juice
1 cup mayonnaise
¹/₂ cup Parmesan cheese
1 cup crushed potato chips

Mix all ingredients, except chips, together and put into greased casserole dish. Top with chips and bake at 450º for 30 minutes.

Red, White, & Blue Salad

Carolyn Wallen

2 boxes red raspberry Jell-O (3-ounce size)
3 cups hot water
1 envelope plain gelatin
1/2 cup water, cold
1 cup coffee cream (liquid form)
1 cup sugar
1 package Philadelphia cream cheese
   (8 ounces), softened
1 teaspoon vanilla
1/2 cup nuts, chopped
1 can blueberries with juice

Allow each layer to set before adding the next one.

First layer: One box Jell-O dissolved in 2 cups hot water.

Middle layer: Dissolve gelatin in 1/2 cup cold water. Heat the cream and sugar without boiling. Mix into gelatin mixture. Whip cheese with mixer. Add gelatin mixture. Add vanilla and nuts, and mix well.

Top layer: Dissolve 1 box raspberry Jell-O in 1 cup hot water. Add berries with juice. Chill until firm.

Carolyn Wallen, Stocking the Park's Bookshelves

On a side street in Gardiner sits a rather nondescript building that blends in with the other half dozen or so buildings on the block. Inside it's even less distinctive—a few desks and Yellowstone ephemera on the walls. For a few minutes the conversation is about what new restaurants have opened in Livingston or Bozeman that would make a trip there worthwhile. But after discussing the small handful of new options, all is serious again, back to serving as the sales office and warehouse for the Yellowstone Association.

A visit to the Yellowstone Association's website (www.yellowstoneassociation.org) will tell you how important this organization is and that its primary mission is to "inspire, educate, and preserve" through exhibits and publications, and that's where Carolyn Wallen comes in. "As warehouse manager, I oversee all the inventory that comes in from vendors all over the country—whether maps, books, games, videos, assorted gift items, puzzles—as long as it's educational," she says. In the summer, the park's high season, she oversees a staff that helps price, shelve, and get inventory out to eight visitor centers as well as to the Lamar campus of the Yellowstone Institute. Every morning a check on the point-of-sale inventory system keeps her posted on what's where in the park. "We fill orders four days a week and deliver them, even in the winter, by snowmobile if needed."

All books must be approved for educational content by the National Park Service. The association carries more than 750 items, the majority of which are books. *Who Pooped in the Park*—a kids' book, is a hot item. "Our bestselling book is one we publish—*The Official Guide to Touring America's First National Park.* Also big sellers are *Yellowstone Trivia, Yellowstone Expedition Guide,* and *Death in Yellowstone,*" she says. Carolyn notes that all their products do well.

The association uses its funds for educational projects, including films and interpretive exhibits, and for protecting the park's archives, publishing interpretive materials, funding scientific research, and for similar projects. Most of the funds come from members' dues and store purchases; a smaller part is from donors. The Yellowstone Association Institute runs programs and classes for just about any natural topic you can imagine: wolves and other park wildlife, hiking, wildflowers, the parks thermal features, fly fishing, wildlife, and even one on hoodoos (don't know what hoodoos are? Stop in at an association bookstore).

All this fits right in with Carolyn's background, not only her education but also the fact that she's lived in more national parks than most people have visited. Her bio reads like a geographic atlas: she was born in California, grew up in Colorado (where she met her husband), secured an elementary education degree, and worked as a teacher's aide while her husband finished school (he now heads the bison management team in Yellowstone). From there it was the Tetons, Redwood National Park, Bryce Canyon, and then Yellowstone. She says, "We're very happy here, not that we weren't elsewhere. The other places weren't bad, but the Rocky Mountains are home to us. I anticipate being here quite a while."

Recipes by Carolyn Wallen

Upper Geyser Basin Chinese Chicken Salad

Jennifer Whipple

Because Asian cuisine was not easily obtainable at the local take-out in the Upper Geyser Basin, I concocted this recipe using ingredients that were easily available (perishables like lettuce and green onions in the winter were ordered from the grocery store in West Yellowstone and then snowcoached into Old Faithful. Occasionally the produce was a little worse for wear, i.e., frozen). The fresh greens were marvelous after eating frozen and canned vegetables all winter.

2 to 4 chicken breasts
1 $10^1/_2$-ounce can chicken broth
2 thick slices gingerroot
$^1/_2$ package rice sticks (maifun)
Salad oil
1 head iceberg lettuce (crunchier!)
4 to 6 green onions, sliced
1 can water chestnuts, sliced (slicing whole
    water chestnuts allows for thinner slices)
$^1/_3$ cup toasted sesame seeds

Cook chicken in chicken broth with the slices of ginger, adding enough water to cover chicken if necessary. Simmer 20 minutes or until chicken is completely cooked. Drain and chill. Shred into bite-sized pieces and refrigerate until needed.

Place rice sticks a few handfuls at a time in $^1/_2$ inch hot oil until puffed. Test oil temperature with a single rice stick—it will puff up significantly when oil is hot enough. Remove rice sticks as cooked and drain on paper towels.

Slice and chop lettuce into bite-sized pieces. Mix lettuce, onions, water chestnuts, sesame seeds (I place them in a cast-iron frying pan and toast on a burner, then use that frying pan to cook rice noodles), rice sticks, and chicken together.

Dressing:

3 tablespoons sugar
1 teaspoon salt
$^3/_4$ teaspoon black pepper
6 tablespoons rice vinegar
$^1/_3$ cup salad oil

Combine sugar, salt, black pepper, and rice vinegar over low heat just until sugar completely dissolved; add salad oil and mix thoroughly.

Toss salad with dressing and serve immediately.

Entrees

4-Bean Casserole

. . . .

Sue & Jack Davis

8 pieces bacon
4 onions
1¼ cups brown sugar
1 tablespoon dry mustard
½ tablespoon garlic salt
½ cup cider vinegar
1 large can B&M baked beans
1 8½-ounce can baby lima beans, drained
2 cans butter beans (drain only 1 can)
1 medium can kidney beans (juice and all)

Cut and fry bacon until crisp; remove from pan, drain, and save bacon fat. Brown onions in pan with bacon fat. Add brown sugar, dry mustard, garlic salt, and vinegar to onions and sauté for 20 minutes.

In a bowl, mix together all the beans. Add onion mixture to the beans and mix together. Pour into 11 x 17 glass baking dish and bake for 1 hour at 300º.

Backpacking Pasta-Roni with White Cheddar & Shells

. . . .

Walter Voeller

*If this is the only meal on your trip that calls for butter, this dish is okay prepared
without the butter, but make sure to take along powdered milk. Plastic screw-top jars
(like those made of Nalgene) are excellent to pack along.
You can premix the butter and milk for this recipe, open it, and dump it all in after the pasta is drained.*

1 package Pasta-Roni with white cheddar
   and shells
Water
Butter
Powdered milk or whipping cream
Fresh red peppers, optional
Mushrooms, optional
Smoked salmon, optional
Parmesan cheese, optional

Make the pasta according to package directions. I like to add fresh red peppers and mushrooms (these two veggies pack as well as most) or smoked salmon and extra Parmesan cheese.

It's really good with whipping cream instead of milk.

Big Sky Venison Tacos

Dianna Kellie

2 pounds ground deer meat or hamburger
2 green peppers, cubed
1 1/2 teaspoons wild game seasoning
1 teaspoon black pepper
1 package large soft flour tortillas
3 cups shredded medium cheddar
   or mozzarella cheese
1 can black olives, sliced
2 cups green onions, sliced
2 large tomatoes, cubed
1/2 head iceberg lettuce, torn into small pieces
1 medium container salsa
Ranch dressing

In large saucepan cook ground meat at medium temperature until done. Add cubed green peppers, reduce heat to low, and add seasonings. Cover and cook for 3 minutes.

On tortilla, spoon on meat, cheese, olives, green onions, tomatoes, and lettuce. Sprinkle salsa on vegetables and meat, drizzle ranch dressing, roll up, and enjoy!

Brunswick Stew (Aunt Olene's Camp Stew)

· · · · · · · · · · · · · · · · · · · ·

Suzanne Lewis

1 large onion, chopped
1 large green pepper, chopped
4 cups frozen cubed hash browns, thawed
1 cup cooked chicken pieces
1 15-ounce can tomato sauce
1 15¼-ounce can lima beans, drained
2 cups chicken broth
¼ teaspoon Worcestershire sauce
1 celery rib, chopped
1 cup frozen sliced okra, thawed
¾ pound BBQ pork, chopped
1 14½-ounce can diced tomatoes, undrained
1 15¼-ounce can whole corn with red
   and green peppers, drained
½ teaspoon salt and pepper each

Combine all ingredients in a 5-quart slow cooker. Cook covered on high for about 6 hours.

Makes 14 cups

Carl's Mad Bear Chili

· · · · · · · · · · · · · · · · · · ·

Carl Sheehan

Carl warns that this is not for the meek. It's delicious served with cornbread.

1 onion, chopped
4 cloves garlic, chopped
1/2 green or red pepper, chopped
1 1/2 pounds hamburger or cubed beef
2 large cans tomatoes, diced
1 can tomato sauce
1 tablespoon salt (scant)
2 to 3 tablespoons chili powder
1 tablespoon cumin
1 tablespoon Worcestershire sauce
1 tablespoon brown sugar
1 tablespoon dark molasses
Black pepper, to taste
1 teaspoon oregano
1 teaspoon bay leaf, if ground, or 1 whole
1 teaspoon marjoram
1 teaspoon lemon juice
1 teaspoon Dijon mustard
1 teaspoon paprika
1 teaspoon basil
1 chili pepper, crushed
Dash of cayenne pepper
1 1/2 cups small red beans
1 can red beans, kidney

Chop and sauté in olive oil, onion, garlic, and green or red pepper. Brown hamburger or cubed meat.

Combine above ingredients with diced tomatoes, tomato sauce, salt, chili powder, cumin, Worcestershire sauce, brown sugar, and dark molasses. Add black pepper to taste.

Add oregano, bay leaf, marjoram, lemon juice, Dijon mustard, paprika, basil, chili pepper, cayenne pepper, red beans, and kidney beans.

Cook 3 to 6 hours, adding water if needed.

Carl's Szechwan Chicken Stir-fry

Carl Sheehan

1 cup soy sauce
2 cubes chicken broth
1 tablespoon brown sugar
$1/2$ teaspoon cayenne pepper
$1/2$ teaspoon ginger
1 teaspoon cornstarch
2 tablespoons water
2 chicken breasts
1 cup red pepper
1 cup snow peas
1 cup onions or scallions
$1/3$ cup garlic, chopped
1 teaspoon ginger, chopped (optional)

Simmer soy sauce, chicken broth, brown sugar, cayenne pepper, and ginger. Add cornstarch mixed with water; stir until thickened.

I grill the chicken breasts quickly. Let them cool, and then cut into cubes.

In a hot wok cook the vegetables, red pepper, snow peas, onions or scallions, garlic, and ginger (optional). Add whatever vegetables are around.

I add chicken last to warm it up and add some sauce to the wok mix before serving.

Serve with rice and the sauce mix.

Carl Sheehan, The Potter at Old Faithful

Carl Sheehan says that in the summer the porch of Old Faithful Lodge is the best place for watching its namesake geyser erupt. Not that you'll often find him sitting there—he's usually busy at his studio inside the lodge, creating distinctive works of clay. He sits at his potter's wheel at one end of the gift shop, surrounded by bowls, mugs, platters, and vases in colors and stylized designs that have become his trademark. Visitors stop to watch him work or to admire one of his finely crafted oil lamps, all of which have his signature and Old Faithful stamped on the bottom. "People look for that," he says.

Years ago while exhibiting his work at a craft show in Bozeman, Carl was approached by a representative of the park's stores. The representative offered to pay Carl for the materials to build a kiln, give him working space in Old Faithful Lodge, and provide him and his family with a cabin for seasonal living. At the time he was teaching part time in Bozeman, "but here was the chance to live and work in Yellowstone—it allowed me the lifestyle I wanted. I love living here and have seen some interesting things. Met two presidents—Carter and Clinton—and was here for the fires in 1988—that was pretty crazy. We had to evacuate in August and couldn't see Old Faithful at times."

Park living has influenced his pottery dramatically. "We have great wildlife. Bison—one of my favorites—are on my pottery. We had a bear at our cabin door once. It went downstream on the Firehole River, crossed the bridge, and looked back at us—I did a piece taken from that." He hints that wolves might appear on future work.

Carl gets his clay—about 1.5 tons at a time—from the Archie Bray Foundation in Helena, Montana, and he and a friend prospect locally for natural material. "We've found some nice terra cotta and a clay that melts into a glaze near Bozeman." He's always experimenting with new glazes but assures that his pieces have no lead and are microwave and dishwasher safe. "I mix my own glazes so I know what's going into them."

Although he often works seven days a week, Carl manages to coach a coed softball team called the Eruptors. "That's my relaxation and fun." But on a more serious, cultural side, he talks of hopes for a Yellowstone art trust. "The plan is that high-caliber artists would come for several weeks and teach at workshops, then leave a piece of art behind so eventually you'd have a nice collection there."

By the end of summer Carl's stock is down to bare bones, so it's back to his home outside Bozeman where he's hardly idle. He teaches classes at the Emerson Cultural Center, exhibits in local galleries and shops, and creates more products and new designs for next year. But come spring you might find him on the porch at the lodge, just long enough to watch Old Faithful erupt before heading inside to his shop and a new season.

Recipes by Carl Sheehan

Chili Mac

. . . .

Dianna Kellie
A family favorite, quick and easy at home or on the trail!

1 large family-size can chili (I prefer Dennison's, but any brand will do)
2 boxes macaroni and cheese dinner
1/2 cup milk
Salt and pepper to taste
1/2 cup shredded cheese of choice

In a large pan, cook macaroni until done; drain. On low heat add chili to macaroni, milk, and 1/4 cup of the grated cheese; cook until contents are hot and cheese is melted. Serve in bowls, and sprinkle remaining cheese on individual portions and salt and pepper to taste.

Chili Rellenos Puff

Carolyn Wallen

1 can (10 ounces) whole green chilies
6 ounces Monterey jack cheese
5 eggs
2/3 cup milk
6 tablespoons flour
3/4 teaspoon baking powder
4 ounces (1 cup) cheddar cheese, shredded
1/4 cup sunflower seeds
1/4 cup pitted black olives, sliced
1 can (15 ounces) tomato sauce, heated

Rinse chilies and pat dry with a paper towel. Slit lengthwise, carefully removing any seeds. Cut cheese into strips just a bit shorter than the chilies, 1/2 inch thick and wide. Place a cheese strip inside each chili, folding chili over to enclose the cheese. Place chilies side by side in well-buttered 8-cup baking dish.

Beat eggs until foamy; beat in milk, flour, and baking powder until smooth. Pour over chilies, moistening all surfaces. Sprinkle cheddar cheese and sunflower seeds over top.

Bake uncovered, in 375º oven for 40 minutes. Remove; let stand 10 minutes before serving.

Garnish with olives and serve with hot tomato sauce.

Curried Chicken

- - - - - - - - - - - - - - - - - - -

Carl Sheehan

1 broiler/fryer chicken, skinned and
   cut into pieces
1 tablespoon butter/oil
1 medium onion, finely chopped
1 teaspoon garlic, minced
2 tablespoons curry powder
1 bay leaf
1 large apple, diced
1 medium banana, diced
2 teaspoons tomato paste
1^1/$_2$ cups chicken broth
Dash garlic powder
Dash cayenne pepper
Dash basil
Dash thyme
Dash parsley
Dash onion powder
Dash pepper
Dash sage
^{1}/$_2$ cup skim milk

Brown chicken in butter or oil.

Add onion, garlic, curry powder, bay leaf, apple, and banana. Cook 5 minutes, and then add tomato paste, chicken broth, and garlic powder, cayenne pepper, basil, thyme, parsley, onion powder, pepper, and sage. When the mixture comes to a boil, reduce heat, cover, and cook for 15 minutes or until tender.

Remove chicken from skillet, set aside and keep warm.

Discard bay leaf.

In a blender/food processor, puree sauce and return to skillet; stir in skim milk, add chicken, and bring sauce to boil.

Serve on rice or noodles.

Flank Steak with Mexican Marinade

· · · · · · · · · · · · · · · · ·

Tara Cross & David Monteith

This marinade is involved but well worth the effort. Also, it can be easily frozen for later use.
The recipe makes enough for one or more steaks.
The heat of the marinade can be controlled by varying the amount of habanero used.
The variety of peppers adds not only heat but a depth of flavor you can't get with just one kind.

Marinade:

1 or 2 habanero peppers
1 or 2 jalapeño peppers
2 Anaheim peppers
2 poblano peppers
1 head garlic peeled
1-inch cube fresh ginger
3 tablespoons cumin seeds
1 tablespoon salt
Black pepper
1 bunch cilantro
16 ounces olive oil (not virgin)
2 oranges
2 lemons
4 limes
2 pounds flank steak
3 large yellow onions sliced into
   3/4-inch-thick rounds
Cooked rice

Marinade should be prepared a day in advance. Roast whole peppers under broiler or over open gas flame until blackened. Place in bag to cool (this steams the pepper and allows you to peel off blackened skin easily). Once cooled, clean peppers. Under running water, remove skin, stem, and seeds.

Warning: thoroughly wash hands after handling peppers. If you have sensitive skin, wear gloves for this process.

In food processor or blender, place peppers, garlic, ginger, cumin seeds, salt, black pepper, cilantro, and 1/4 cup oil. Grind into paste. Place into large heat-resistant bowl, allowing at least 4 inches of space above paste.

Heat remaining olive oil to near smoking. Carefully pour oil over paste. Please use caution: paste will

Let cool 10 minutes.

While cooling, juice citrus fruit (recipe needs about 2 cups of juice total). Once marinade has cooled, add juice and stir.

In a nonreactive container, marinate flank steak in 1 cup of marinade for 2 hours (and up to a day).

When ready to cook, remove excess marinade from flank steak. Cook flank steak and onion slices over hot grill or broiler until steak is medium-rare. Thinly slice steak on bias across grain.

Gently heat remaining unused marinade over low heat. Serve steak with onions, rice, and warmed marinade.

Recipes by Tara Cross & David Monteith

Tara Cross, Geyser Gazer

Tara Cross came to Yellowstone for the first time when she was four months old. Nine years later she became interested in geysers. Now she's one of about 150 regular geyser gazers who spend every possible minute in the park's geyser basins. Geyser gazers are pretty easy to recognize; their "uniform" is simple—a rainproof jacket and brimmed hat. But it's the chattering on their radios as they hike the boardwalks, faces intent, that clinches their identification.*

For most of them, geyser gazing is a hobby. Although they represent all occupations, many are in education and are able to spend summers in Yellowstone. Gazers know every geyser by name and habit, and they record data religiously—from the day and time of an eruption to how long it lasts. All the information is given to the National Park Service. Tara says that's how a ranger figured out the eruption pattern for Old Faithful.

According to guidebooks, the Upper Geyser Basin is home to 300 to 400 of the park's 10,000-plus thermal features. Tara says by definition the number of thermal features in the Upper Geyser Basin is more like 1,000. "This is the most active geyser area in the world," she notes, "and Grand is the world's tallest predictable geyser." Grand's eruptions can go 200 feet high, and there are bleachers for visitors to sit and watch it. "Nowhere else will you find as many big geysers connected to each other. For example, Daisy geyser suddenly went to 90-minute intervals when the earthquake happened in Alaska, and the 1959 Hebgen Lake earthquake had a dramatic effect on the park's geysers."

Aside from gathering data, geyser gazing is about camaraderie. "I have many good friends here," Tara says. "We have a lot of downtime just waiting, so we fraternize." That's how she met David Monteith. "I knew him for several years as a fellow gazer, but we started dating and two years later were married." They had planned to marry at Riverside Geyser but weather forced them indoors to Old Faithful Lodge. "After the wedding we walked out to find Castle Geyser erupting. Daisy and Grand joined in a few minutes later, and then Beehive (it erupts only once a day). On our way back from watching Beehive, Old Faithful erupted right on cue. We couldn't have asked for more!"

Like many gazers, Tara has personal park history: she's worked here and as an accomplished violinist (began when she was five), she played at Old Faithful Inn with pianist George Sanborn. "I play mostly in symphonies but I just loved playing at the inn. I even played there for family and friends the night before my wedding."

Tara's radio suddenly crackles with news from an *oblophile* (the gazers' pet name for a person who watches Oblong Geyser) and she heads off down the boardwalk.

*Like any specialty group, there's an organization to accommodate it: GOSA (Geyser Observation and Study Association). Tara's husband, David Monteith, started GOSA's website (http://geyserstudy.computerpoint.net), which has everything one could want to know about geysers: annual data, glossary, world geyser sites, a webcam to watch Old Faithful, and more.

Hot Chicken Salad en Casserole

Tom & Bonnie Murphy

This recipe is from my Grandmother Griffith's old cookbook from a women's club in Iowa.
I doubled this recipe for 10 people and could have used even more.

2 cups diced chicken
2 cups chopped celery
$1/2$ cup almond flakes
  (toasted for 5 minutes at 400º)
$1/3$ cup chopped green pepper
2 tablespoons minced green onion
$1/2$ teaspoon salt
2 tablespoons lemon juice
1 cup mayonnaise
2 cups crushed potato chips
$1/3$ cup grated cheese

Blend chicken, celery, almonds, green pepper, onion, salt, lemon juice, and mayo. Put alternate layers of chicken mixture and crushed potato chips in buttered casserole. Top with layer of chips and grated cheese mixed together. Bake at 350º for about 20 to 30 minutes.

Kenny's Fireplace Trout

Walter Voeller

This works well at home on a grill or in the backcountry over a fire.

18-inch fresh brown trout
Lemon juice
Butter
Fresh garlic
Fresh onion
Hot sauce
Cilantro

Wrap the trout in foil with lemon juice, butter, garlic, onion, sprinkles of hot sauce, and cilantro stuffed into body cavity.

Place the foil-wrapped trout on hot coals right in the fireplace or on a grill for 8 minutes on each side. It will take slightly less time for smaller trout.

It's done when it easily flakes off bones.

An 18-inch brown from Lewis Lake will serve two.

Lamb Chops with Spiced Salt

Suzanne Lewis

This is my husband's recipe. It goes well with any meat.

3 tablespoons coriander seeds
2 tablespoons fennel seeds
2 tablespoons fine sea salt
1 tablespoon dried thyme
$1/2$ tablespoon coarse ground pepper
6 lamb chops (6-8 ounces each)

In a blender, whirl coriander seeds and fennel seeds until finely ground. Add sea salt, dried thyme, and coarse ground pepper; whirl to combine.

Rub about $1/2$ teaspoon salt mixture into each lamb chop. Wrap airtight and chill for at least 4 hours or up to 1 day.

Unwrap chops, pour 1 tablespoon vegetable oil into a 10- or 12-inch nonstick pan over medium-high heat and swirl to coat. Add chops and cook 8 to 12 minutes.

Lamb Meatballs

. . . .

Jack & Tina Gilchrist

Tina raises blue-ribbon sheep that give not only great meatballs but also prize fleeces that she spins, weaves, and dyes. You might see Jack sporting one of her wool hats while bear watching.

1 10³/₄-ounce can cheese soup
¹/₂ can water and ¹/₂ can milk
1 egg, slightly beaten
1 pound ground lamb or beef
¹/₃ cup uncooked rice
¹/₄ cup chopped onion
1 teaspoon salt
¹/₄ teaspoon oregano and dash pepper

Dilute soup with water and milk, then add only ¹/₃ cup soup mix, egg, and other ingredients to meat. Form into 20 balls and brown. Pour remaining soup over meatballs; cover and simmer or bake 30 to 35 minutes or until rice is tender. If sauce is too thick, add extra milk, and heat.

Lentil Burgers

Doug Smith

Doug created these for the backcountry but says they're equally good at home.

Lentils, soaked 4 to 6 hours
1 or 2 eggs
Breadcrumbs, unflavored
1 package onion soup mix
Raw onion, chopped

Boil lentils 30 minutes, drain water. Mix in eggs, breadcrumbs, soup mix, and onion.

Make into patties and fry.

Good with mayonnaise, mustard, and ketchup—or for a dressed-up burger, add cheese, tomato, avocado slice, onion, or a slice of pineapple.

NOTE: It's a good idea to soak the lentils when you leave for work in the morning, but if you forgot, you can boil them about 40 minutes without presoaking.

Macaroni and Cheese Soufflé

Bob Richard

This comes from one of my guests from Georgia. It's wonderful.

1¹/2 cups macaroni
2 cups milk
3 eggs, lightly whisked
1/2 pound sharp cheddar cheese, grated
2/3 (or less) stick butter or margarine, melted
White pepper
Salt

Cook macaroni in salted boiling water for 7 to 8 minutes; drain. Add milk, eggs, cheese, butter, pepper, and salt. Layer or mix all together.

Bake 25 to 30 minutes at 350°. Serve immediately.

Mama Bear's Lasagna

Carl Sheehan

1 pound sweet Italian sausage
1 pound ground beef
2 cloves garlic, minced
1 tablespoon dried basil
Dash salt
1 can (28 ounces) diced tomatoes
1 can (15 ounces) tomato sauce
1 can (6 ounces) tomato paste
1/2 cup dry red wine/cooking sherry
10 to 12 ounces lasagna noodles, cooked
2 eggs, beaten
3 cups ricotta or cottage cheese
1/2 cup Parmesan cheese, grated
2 tablespoons parsley flakes
1/2 teaspoon salt
1/8 teaspoon pepper
1 pound part-skim mozzarella cheese, grated

Brown, sausage and beef; drain fat. Add garlic, basil, salt, tomatoes, tomato sauce, tomato paste, and wine/sherry. Simmer uncovered 30 minutes, stirring often.

Beat eggs and add ricotta cheese, Parmesan cheese, parsley flakes, salt, and pepper.

Preheat oven to 375º.

Spread small amount of sauce in bottom of 13 x 9 x 2 inch pan to prevent sticking.

Layer 3 or 4 lasagna noodles, a third of ricotta mixture, a third of mozzarella, and a third of meat sauce. Repeat two more times and top with sprinkle of Parmesan.

Bake 30 minutes or until bubbly.

Marinated Niman Ranch Pork Chops with Stir-fried Cabbage

....

OLD FAITHFUL INN
Chef Jim Chapman

8 5-ounce pork chops
1¼ cups peanut oil
1 teaspoon dry mustard
1 teaspoon minced garlic
1 tablespoon chopped fresh rosemary
1 tablespoon minced shallot
½ teaspoon salt
¼ teaspoon pepper
1 tablespoon caraway seeds
1 pound shredded cabbage
¼ cup cider vinegar
Salt and pepper to taste

Marinate pork chops with 1 cup oil, mustard, garlic, rosemary, shallots, salt, and pepper for at least 4 hours.

Drain pork chops and grill.

While cooking pork chops heat ¼ cup oil in sauté pan and toast caraway seeds until aromatic; add cabbage and toss until heated. Add vinegar and let steam for 30 seconds. Finish with salt and pepper.

Yield 4 portions

Jim Chapman, Master of Menus

Foodies think of Emeril and New Orleans, Wolfgang Puck and Hollywood, and Jim Chapman and Yellowstone. No? Well, they should, because Jim cooks and designs menus that make these other guys look like short-order cooks. And he does it for about 1.5 million people a year because Jim is executive chef of Yellowstone's restaurants.

Before landing in Wyoming, this Connecticut native worked at several different restaurant jobs to pay his way through the University of Connecticut as a computer science major. After only one semester, he realized he had more fun cooking and four years later enrolled at the Culinary Institute of America (CIA).

For the next 25 years he cooked his way from New England to Switzerland to Mississippi, where during an Internet surf he saw the job listing for Yellowstone. Jim and his wife, Suzanne, had been to Yellowstone in 1996 and loved it, so he applied. His interview with Xanterra Parks & Resorts™ (the park's food and beverage and lodging concessionaire) consisted of a mystery basket with assorted food items from which he had to prepare a four-course meal for 15 people. He was hired.

Xanterra's and Jim's philosophy of sustainable cuisine was a perfect match. "Sustainability is meeting today's needs without compromising the ability of future generations to meet their own needs," Jim says. "We use organic and natural local products: pork from Livingston, lentils from Conrad, Flathead Lake fish, Red Lodge beef, and Wyoming and Montana cherries." The Alaskan salmon is Marine Stewardship Council certified, which means that it comes from sustainable-practice fisheries. The same philosophy goes for swordfish—"We don't use it because it's overfished, along with several other species identified by the Montery Bay Aquarium Seafood Watch program."

Jim often spends more time writing menus and creating recipes than cooking, unless there's a special function. "The park's recipes change but popular items such as prime rib and Idaho trout tend to stick around," he says.

"One of the big things I have going on now is as a member of the American Culinary Federation we're in the process of starting an apprentice program in the park," Jim says. It's a three-year program that entails 6,000 hours of on-the-job training and 600 classroom hours—an alternative to going to a culinary institute. "I'm really excited about it."

On the home front, Jim does all the cooking and Suzanne cleans up, which keeps her stepping because the CIA stresses clean as you go. As the bottle washer, she's amazed at how many pans a chef can use—"things that aren't even meant to be pans," she says.

Unlike some chefs who privately pig out on DingDongs, Jim's favorite food and his preference for a last meal would be a nice filet mignon with seared fois gras, topped with a little Madeira sauce—very decadent, very rich. But as a last meal on a budget, it would be roast chicken correctly done with herbs, seasonings, and butter.

Jim puts in incredibly long hours and you'll seldom find him in his office, but he says, "It's my dream job. I love it."

Recipes by Chef Jim Chapman

Montana Fried Trout

· · · · · · · · · · · · · · · · · · ·

Dianna Kellie

These are great served with a vegetable and salad. After placing fillets on plate, sprinkle a touch of paprika for color and add a sprig of parsley and lemon wedge on the side for a nice presentation.

4 large fresh trout fillets
2 tablespoons butter or margarine
Salt and pepper to taste
$1/2$ lemon cut into wedges
$1/8$ cup tiny slivered almonds
Paprika
Parsley sprigs

In a large frying pan, heat butter or margarine until melted. Use medium low to medium heat—you don't want to overcook the fish. Add trout fillets, pepper, and a little salt.

While fish are cooking, squeeze a little lemon on them. Turn fillets, season, and add more lemon juice. Add almonds, reduce heat, cover pan, and cook 5 to 7 minutes more, or until fish are done to your liking.

Mother's Chicken

Lee Whittlesey

10 to 12 small chicken thighs
   (or 4 or 5 chicken breasts)
Seasoned salt
Paprika
3 chicken bouillon cubes
1$^1/_2$ cups water
$^3/_8$ teaspoon minced onion
$^3/_8$ teaspoon curry powder
2 tablespoons cooking wine
Mushrooms for gravy

Cover chicken with seasoned salt and paprika. Dissolve bouillon cubes in water. Add minced onion, curry powder, and cooking wine. Bring to a boil.

Pour over chicken and bake covered at 350° for 30 minutes. Uncover and bake 45 minutes.

To make gravy, add pan juices to flour and water, then add mushrooms.

Mudpot Stroganoff

Jennifer Whipple

This dish when done is reminiscent of a mudpot cheerfully bubbling away.

2 pounds round steak cut in 1/2-inch strips
1/4 cup salad oil
1 tablespoon salt
1/2 teaspoon pepper
1/2 cup dry red wine
1 cup thinly sliced onions
   (approximately 1 large onion)
2 cups thinly sliced fresh mushrooms
3 tablespoons flour
1 6-ounce can tomato paste
1 can (10 1/2 ounces) beef consommé
1 bay leaf crumbled
1 clove garlic, minced

Brown meat quickly in oil, then transfer to a 3-quart casserole; add salt, pepper, and wine.

In the drippings of the frying pan, sauté the onions until golden brown, add the mushrooms, and cook an additional 5 minutes. Sprinkle flour over mushrooms and onions, carefully stirring it in; then add tomato paste, consommé, bay leaf, and garlic. Mix well and pour over meat.

Cover and bake in a 350° oven for 1 hour or until meat is tender. Serve over rice or noodles with sour cream.

Oriental Chicken Thighs

· · · · · · · · · · · · · · · · · · ·

Tara Cross & David Monteith

This is an easy and forgiving dish that packs good flavor.

8 chicken thighs

Marinade:

4 ounces Hoisin sauce
2 tablespoons rice vinegar
2 tablespoons soy sauce
2 cloves garlic, minced
2 teaspoons fresh ginger, minced
3 green onions, minced
Ground black pepper

Steamed rice

Mix marinade ingredients. Dredge chicken thighs in marinade. Cook over medium-high grill until done or for about 40 minutes in 375° oven. Baste every 10 minutes with extra marinade. Move chicken to keep from sticking. Turn once during cooking. If cooking in oven, during last 5 minutes, turn skin-side up and increase heat to 400° in order to crisp skin. Serve with steamed rice.

Outback Stir-fry with Rice or Couscous

Walter Voeller

This is better on a shorter, lightweight packing trip and for two or three people, otherwise you'd need to carry more ingredients and a bigger, heavier pan.

Sugar peas or green beans
Broccoli, chopped
Bell pepper, chopped
Yellow crookneck squash, chopped
Mushrooms, clean and trim
2 to 4 tablespoons oil
Bean sprouts
Boil-in-bag brown rice
Soy or oyster sauce

For this dish, it's good to have two stoves, one to boil the rice and the other for stir-frying (you can stir-fry over a fire).

Cook harder/bigger or denser vegetables first (like broccoli or cauliflower or green beans) then add softer and smaller things. Add bean sprouts just before taking off heat.

This basic stir-fry needs a sauce to liven it up. The lightest is the soy, Parmesan, and pizza pepper packet blend (or take a bottle of oyster sauce).

Pan Seared Veal Chops w/ Citron Sauce & Mushroom Risotto

· · · · · · · · · · · · · · · · · ·

LAKE HOTEL
Chef Jim Chapman

Veal Chop:

2 tablespoons olive oil
4 10-ounce Frenched veal rib chops
Salt and pepper, to taste

Citron Sauce:

1 ounce butter
1 ounce flour
1 tablespoon shallots minced
$1/2$ cup white wine
1 cup chicken broth or stock
1 cup heavy cream
$1/4$ cup lemon juice
$1/8$ teaspoon turmeric

Mushroom Risotto:

$51/2$ cups chicken stock or broth
1 ounce butter
1 tablespoon shallots, minced
2 cloves garlic, minced
2 ounces shiitake mushrooms, sliced
2 ounces portabella mushrooms, diced,
    gills removed
$13/4$ cups Arborio rice
1 cup white wine
$1/4$ cup heavy cream
$1/4$ cup Parmesan cheese
1 tablespoon parsley, chopped

For the Veal Chop:

Heat oil in a heavy-bottomed skillet. Season veal chops with salt and pepper; sear chops until golden brown, and finish in 350° oven.

For Citron Sauce:

Make roux by melting butter and whisking in flour. Cook for 2 minutes and let cool.

In a saucepan combine shallots and white wine; simmer until reduced by half. Add stock, cream, lemon juice, and turmeric, and bring to a boil. Whisk in roux and let simmer for 2 minutes.

For Mushroom Risotto:

Heat broth and keep hot. Melt butter; sauté shallots and garlic, and do not brown. Add mushrooms and sauté 3 minutes. Add rice and stir to coat. Add $1/2$ cup broth, stirring constantly until dry. Add another $1/2$ cup of broth and cook, stirring until dry. Repeat until all broth is used, about 25 minutes. Finish with white wine, cream, Parmesan, and parsley.

Yield 4 portions

Pasta Soufflé

. . . .

Tara Cross & David Monteith

Almost any vegetable you like can be used in place of or in addition to mushrooms:
steamed broccoli or sautéed spinach, for example.

2¹/₂ cups milk
¹/₄ cup finely diced onion
1 bay leaf
2 thyme sprigs
5 tablespoons butter
3¹/₂ tablespoons flour
Salt
Pepper
Pinch grated nutmeg
1 pound button mushrooms, quartered
1 tablespoon butter
1 tablespoon oil
3 eggs, separated
¹/₂ cup grated Swiss cheese
¹/₂ cup grated Parmesan cheese
8 ounces angel hair pasta, cooked
Grated Parmesan cheese for topping

Preheat oven to 450º.

Heat milk, onion, bay leaf, and thyme over medium heat. Turn off just before it comes to boil. Let rest 15 minutes. Remove bay leaf.

In another saucepan, melt 5 tablespoons butter. Add flour and stir over medium heat for 2 minutes until flour is cooked. Stir in milk mixture, and whisk until smooth. Cook over low heat for 20 minutes, stirring occasionally to prevent sticking. Season with salt, pepper, and nutmeg.

Sauté mushrooms over high heat in 1 tablespoon butter and 1 tablespoon oil until juices are rendered and mushrooms begin to brown. Season with salt and pepper.

Butter 2-quart soufflé or gratin dish, or steep-sided bowl.

Wisk a little of the sauce into the egg yolks to temper them. Mix egg yolks, cheeses, and mushrooms into remaining sauce.

Whip egg whites until they hold stiff peaks. In a large bowl, mix ¹/₄ egg whites into sauce to loosen sauce. Carefully fold sauce into remaining egg whites. Fold in pasta. Transfer to cooking dish. Sprinkle top with grated Parmesan. Bake until puffed and golden, about 25 minutes.

Pecan Chicken

. . . .

Bob Richard

Pecans tend to turn things blue, so add them at the last minute.
I usually make this dish in a Dutch oven over a campfire.

4 7-ounce chicken breasts, boneless
Mustard butter (2 parts butter,
    1 part Dijon mustard, blended)
Pecans, crushed
3 ounces clarified butter
4 ounces sour cream
2 ounces Dijon mustard
2 ounces cream

The night before:
Brush the chicken breasts with mustard butter.

Roll in crushed pecans, then sauté in butter until golden brown. Remove from pan to plate. Drain excess fat from pan. Add sour cream, mustard, and cream to pan. Whisk together and pour over chicken breasts.

Pork Stew with Mushrooms & White Wine

Tom & Bonnie Murphy

One of Tom's clients sent me this recipe, knowing it would travel well.
As with so many dishes of this type, it tastes even better the next day.

2¹/₂ pounds boneless pork
1 tablespoon oil
1 tablespoon butter
2 onions, chopped
2 tablespoons flour
1 cup dry white wine
2 cups chicken broth
3 shallots, chopped
2 tomatoes, peeled, seeded, and chopped
   (or a 1-pound can, drained)
1 bay leaf, 2 thyme springs, 2 parsley sprigs
2 cloves garlic, minced
Salt and pepper
³/₄ pound mushrooms, quartered

Cut the pork into 1¹/₂-inch cubes. In a heavy casserole, heat the oil and butter and fry the pork until thoroughly browned on all sides. Remove the pork, add the onions and brown them. Stir in the flour and brown it, too. Note: It is the thorough browning that gives flavor to the stew. Add wine and bring to a boil. Stir in chicken broth, spices, shallots, tomatoes, garlic, salt and pepper, and pork. Cover the casserole, bring to a boil, then bake in a 350º oven for 1 to 1¹/₂ hours until the pork is tender. Stir occasionally and add stock if necessary. Add mushrooms and continue to cook until mushrooms are tender and meat is almost falling apart. If sauce is too thin, boil to reduce.

Pork'n Apples with Rice

. . . .

Jack & Tina Gilchrist

This was cheap to make in 1967 in Missouri and a requirement for grad student days.

4 pork chops
1 teaspoon salt
1/4 teaspoon pepper
1 20-ounce can pie-sliced apples
1 tablespoon lemon juice
1 tablespoon brown sugar
1 cup rice, uncooked
1 tablespoon instant onion
1/2 teaspoon crushed rosemary
2 teaspoons instant beef bouillon or 2 cubes
2 cups boiling water

Heat oven to 400°.

Brown chops in pan; add salt and pepper. Place in casserole and add apples with lemon juice and brown sugar. Combine rice with onions and rosemary; sprinkle around meat. Dissolve bouillon in boiling water; pour over rice and meat. Spread apples over the rice and chops. Cover and bake 45 minutes or until rice is cooked and pork is tender.

Rhea's Meatloaf

Bob Richard

This is my mother's recipe and the best ever. It's good hot or cold

3/4 pound ham
1 1/2 pounds lean beef
2 cups soft breadcrumbs
1 3/4 teaspoons salt
1/8 teaspoon pepper
1/4 teaspoon mustard
2 eggs
1 1/4 cups milk
1/2 cup brown sugar
1/4 teaspoon cinnamon
1/4 teaspoon cloves
1/8 teaspoon nutmeg

Grind together ham and beef. Mix together breadcrumbs, salt, pepper, mustard, eggs, and milk. Mix with ground meat. Mix brown sugar, cinnamon, cloves, and nutmeg and place in bottom of baking pan. Put meat on top.

Bake 1 1/2 hours at 350°.

Rice with Chilies & Cheese

Carolyn Wallen

3 cups rice, cooked
1 teaspoon oregano leaf, crushed (or to taste)
Salt and pepper, to taste
1 can (7 ounces) green chilies, diced
   and drained
1 can (2$^1/_2$ ounces) pimientos, diced
   and drained
$^1/_2$ pint dairy sour cream
$^1/_2$ pound (2 cups) mild cheddar cheese, grated
Chopped chives, diced pimientos and
   paprika for garnish

Combine rice, oregano, salt, and pepper. Mix lightly but thoroughly.

Combine chilies and pimientos, if used, with sour cream. In a well-greased, round casserole (1$^1/_2$-quart size) add about a third of the rice. Spoon about half of the sour cream mixture on top of the rice. Sprinkle about half of the cheese on the sour cream mixture.

Add in layers, another third of the rice, remaining sour cream mixture, and nearly all the remaining cheese. Reserve some cheese for top.

Add a layer of remaining rice on top. Sprinkle with some of the reserved cheese.

Bake, covered in oven preheated to 350° about 20 minutes. Uncover and sprinkle remaining reserved cheese on top. Bake about 10 minutes longer or until cheese is bubbly.

Garnish with chives, pimiento, and paprika.

Makes 6 servings

Roasted Black Cod with Stewed Vine-Ripened Tomatoes, White Truffle Oil, & Cauliflower Sauce

OLD FAITHFUL INN
Chef Jim Chapman

1 teaspoon chopped garlic
1 ounce olive oil
4 vine-ripened tomatoes peeled, seeded, and chopped
Salt, to taste
White pepper, to taste
1 teaspoon chopped fresh basil
2 ounces butter
2 ounces flour
2 cups heavy cream
2 cups light chicken stock
1/2 head cauliflower cut into small florets
1 1/2 pounds black cod fillets
2 ounces vegetable oil
4 teaspoons white truffle oil

Sauté garlic in olive oil without browning; add tomatoes and reduce to low temperature and cover. Let stew until tomatoes are very soft. Add salt and pepper to taste and finish with fresh basil right before service. Should not be runny.

Melt butter and add flour to make roux; cook for 3 minutes and let cool.

Combine cream, stock, and cauliflower; bring to boil and reduce to simmer. Cook until cauliflower is soft; puree in blender, then return to pan. Whisk in cold roux and return to boil. Add more salt and pepper to taste and adjust for consistency and seasoning. Pass through fine strainer.

Portion cod into four 6-ounce pieces; coat with vegetable oil and season with salt and pepper. Place on rack in roasting pan and bake at 400° for conventional oven or 350° for convection oven until internal temperature of 140° (approximately 10 minutes).

Pool cauliflower sauce on plate, place cod on top of sauce, spoon dollop of stewed tomatoes on top of cod, and drizzle with 1 teaspoon white truffle oil.

Yield 4 portions

Scorpion Pasta

. . . .

Ruth & Leslie Quinn

1 pound chicken
4 cloves garlic, chopped
8 ounces penne pasta
4 tablespoons butter
4 tablespoons flour
2+ cups low-fat milk
2 tablespoons chopped jalapeño peppers
1 tablespoon jalapeño juice or
   hot pepper sauce
1 cup shredded Parmesan cheese

Cut chicken into small pieces and cook in a little bit of oil until done. Add chopped garlic toward the end of cooking and cook until garlic is lightly browned. Dish into large serving bowl.

Separately, boil pasta in water until tender and add to serving bowl.

Prepare a white sauce in a small saucepan by stirring flour into melted butter. Make a smooth paste and cook on medium heat, bubbling for a minute or so. Slowly add milk, a little at a time, until blended, stirring constantly. Continue cooking until mixture thickens, then add peppers, juice or sauce, and cheese. Toss this mixture into the already prepared meat and pasta.

Spaghetti Sauce with Tomato, Orange, & Basil

Tara Cross & David Monteith

Tara notes that husband, David, supplied all her recipes.
To get the most out of this recipe, try one of his variations.

1 tablespoon butter
1 tablespoon olive oil
$1/8$ to $1/4$ teaspoon cayenne pepper
2 leeks (white part only, chopped)
3 cloves garlic (chopped)
2 16-ounce cans tomatoes
2 oranges (grated zest—the orange part only of the rind—of 2 oranges)
$3/4$ to 1 teaspoon salt
Black pepper
$1/4$ cup fresh basil (cut into thin strips)
16 ounces dried spaghetti

In a three-quart saucepan over medium-high heat, melt butter, oil, and cayenne. Once butter has melted, add leeks and sauté until translucent. Add garlic and sauté 1 minute more. Add tomatoes, grated orange zest, salt, and pepper. Reduce heat to medium-low, and gently simmer uncovered for 40 minutes.

Cook spaghetti according to package directions.

While spaghetti is cooking, run tomato sauce through a food mill. Return sauce to saucepan, discarding solids. Add basil to sauce and gently heat. Correct seasoning.

Serve over spaghetti, with side salad and garlic bread.

Variations:

1. Replace orange zest with grated zest of two lemons.

2. Sauté 1 pound quartered button mushrooms in butter and oil. Add to sauce just before serving.

3. For a chunkier and less intense sauce, don't run through food mill.

4. Serve with mild Italian sausage links

Sweet & Savory Ribs

· · · · · · · · · · · · · · · · ·

Carolyn Wallen

1 large onion, sliced and separated into rings
2¹/₂ to 3 pounds boneless country-style
   pork or beef ribs
1 (18 ounces) bottle honey barbecue sauce
¹/₃ cup maple syrup
¹/₄ cup spicy brown mustard
¹/₂ teaspoon salt
¹/₄ teaspoon pepper

Place onion in a 5-quart slow cooker. Top with the ribs. Combine the barbecue sauce, syrup, mustard, salt, and pepper and pour over ribs.

Cover and cook on low 8 to 9 hours or until the meat is tender.

Upper Geyser Basin Wild Game Pot Roast

Dianna Kellie

Leftover roast sliced for sandwiches makes a great picnic lunch when you visit Yellowstone!

1 large moose or elk roast (beef works well, too)
$1/2$ teaspoon pepper
$1/4$ teaspoon garlic salt
$1/2$ teaspoon wild game seasoning salt
4 large potatoes
1 pint garden carrots or store bought
1 can stewed tomatoes
2 teaspoons all-seasoning salt

In a large roaster pan add 2 inches water. Place roast in center of pan and season with pepper, garlic salt, and wild game seasoning salt. Cube potatoes, slice carrots, and add tomatoes in the areas around the roast. Don't pile vegetables on top of roast. Add all-seasoning salt to vegetables. Cook at 300º for $2^1/_2$ hours. Check roast and vegetables every half hour and baste if necessary. Use foil to cover and leave a small area open to vent steam during cooking.

Walnut Chicken

. . . .

Carolyn Wallen
This goes well with wild game.

1 1/2 cups rice, uncooked
1 cup walnuts
3 tablespoons oil
2 green peppers cut into strips
2 carrots, sliced diagonally
2 cups chicken cut into strips
2 tablespoons cornstarch
1 teaspoon sugar
1/2 teaspoon salt
1/2 teaspoon ginger
1/2 teaspoon red pepper, crushed
3 tablespoons soy sauce
4 green onions, sliced diagonally

Prepare rice. Stir-fry walnuts in hot oil until golden; remove from pan. Stir-fry green peppers and carrots until crisp tender; remove and set aside. Stir-fry chicken.

Combine cornstarch, sugar, salt, ginger, pepper, and soy sauce. Add to chicken in pan along with walnuts, green peppers, carrots, and green onions. Toss together until thoroughly coated.

Serve over cooked rice.

Wild Alaskan Salmon Poached in Court Bouillon with Cucumbers, Tomato, & Dill

OLD FAITHFUL INN
Chef Jim Chapman

1¹/₂ pounds wild Alaskan salmon fillets
¹/₂ gallon Court Bouillon (recipe follows)
2 cucumbers
2 tomatoes
1 cup white wine
2 tablespoons chopped shallots
2 cups crème fraiche or sour cream
Salt and white pepper to taste
2 tablespoons chopped fresh dill

Portion salmon into four 6-ounce pieces. Heat Court Bouillon to 180º (just below a simmer). Peel cucumbers, split lengthwise, scoop out seeds with a spoon, and slice into ¹/₄-inch crescents.

Peel, seed, and dice tomatoes. Prepare tomatoes by scooping out core and scoring an X on the other end; drop tomato into boiling water for 15 seconds, then shock in cold water. Skin will peel off easily with paring knife. Cut tomato in half crosswise; squeeze and scoop out seeds; dice into ¹/₄-inch cubes.

Place fish in pan with Court Bouillon; do not stack. Cook until done (fish will be firm, not mushy) about 12 minutes, but time will vary with the thickness of the fillets.

While fish is poaching make sauce by reducing white wine with shallots by half. Add crème fraiche and bring to simmer. Add cucumbers and diced tomatoes; season with salt and pepper. Check taste and consistency, and finish with chopped dill right before serving with white rice or boiled potatoes.

Court Bouillon

¹/₂ gallon water
4 ounces white wine vinegar
4 ounces onion, sliced
2 ounces celery, sliced
2 ounces carrots, sliced
1 ounce salt
¹/₄ teaspoon peppercorns
1 bay leaf
¹/₈ ounce fresh thyme on branch
5 or 6 parsley stems

Combine all ingredients in saucepot and bring to boil. Reduce heat and simmer for 30 minutes. Strain and cool or keep hot if using right away.

Yield 4 portions

Joe Mitchell, Gear Jammer

Ask park employees if they know Joe Mitchell and they'll hesitate, but mention Popeye and many will remember the tour bus driver as though it were yesterday. When he began working for the park in 1947 he was known as Little Joe, but from his habit of smoking a corncob pipe, the nickname "Popeye" stuck. "I wasn't crazy about that—I don't even like spinach," he laughs.

After high school Joe left Billings for Detroit to make airplane motors for Cadillac. Back home—the company on strike and Joe on leave of absence—he noticed an ad for bus drivers in Yellowstone, so he practiced double clutching on his mother's car and passed the test. "My leave expired, and I got an extension. Then each year I'd get another leave to go back to the park." This on-again, off-again relationship continued for years. When Cadillac would no longer give him time off, Joe quit and went to work for the Northern Pacific Railroad where he was given a leave every summer for "personal reasons." He retired from the park and the railroad after juggling schedules for nearly 35 years.

"Of course, things were much different then. I wore a uniform—badge, cap, and park jacket. We'd pick up the people and tell them about the park, but because the buses were so noisy, we were issued bullhorns so we could be heard, but they were useless. On cold days we'd hand out woolen blankets—the only heat in the buses."

Bus drivers were known as "gear jammers," and they were issued their own buses to drive and maintain. Joe considers himself lucky to never have had an accident or breakdown with bus number 204. One time Joe was asked to take Lady Bird Johnson to the top of Mount Washburn. "To this day other drivers still don't believe I got the big new motor coach bus up there—it's not built for that."

Fried trout à la Maytag

Joe Mitchell doesn't have a recipe in this book, but he did use an interesting piece of cooking equipment. One of the benefits of his job was that Joe could spend every spare minute fishing in blue-ribbon trout streams. Joe says, "I had a frying pan made from an old Maytag washing machine lid. The aluminum lid was light and easy to carry for cooking and eating on the spot."

Sides

Dilly Beans

- - - - - - - - - - - - - - - - - - - -

Barbara Forbes Rinker

This recipe was given to us by our daughter, Cynthia Petera, who got it from her husband's Grandma Reynolds from Sundance, Wyoming.

Wash 2 pint jars. (Do not have to be sealed canning jars.)

To the empty jars add:

> ¹/₄ teaspoon crushed red pepper
> 1 head dill or 1 teaspoon dill seed
> 1 clove of garlic, chopped

Pack green beans (washed) into jars until no more can fit. Set aside.

In a pan combine:

> 2 cups vinegar
> 1 cup water
> 2 tablespoons of canning salt

Bring to a boil. Pour over beans and fill to top of jars. Put on lids and refrigerate overnight.

Onion Pie

Sue & Jack Davis

Most of Sue's recipes come from her mother, "the food pusher—as soon as you'd walk in the door, she wanted to feed you." This is equally good as a side dish or main course with a salad.

1¹/₂ cups saltine crackers
¹/₄ cup plus 2 tablespoons margarine, melted
3 cups chopped onion
3 tablespoons butter
3 eggs
1 cup plus 2 tablespoons milk
Salt and pepper
¹/₄ cup plus 2 tablespoons sharp cheese, grated
Paprika

Crush saltines finely. Melt the margarine and mix in with cracker crumbs. Line a 9-inch pie pan with the mixture.

In a frying pan, sauté the onion in 3 tablespoons butter until soft, not brown. In a medium bowl, beat the eggs slightly with the milk, and add a dash of salt and pepper. Stir onion gently into milk mixture, then pour into cracker-lined pan. Top with the cheese and sprinkle with paprika.

Bake 30 minutes at 350° (center will firm up some).

Oven Roast Potatoes

. . . .

Bob Richard

For more flavor and nutrition, don't peel the potatoes. Smaller new potatoes require less baking time.

3/4 cup butter
10 large baking potatoes, about 5 pounds
1 1/2 tablespoons coarse seasoned Hawaiian salt
3/4 cup canned chicken broth, consommé,
   or beef broth
Seasoned grilling salt

Preheat oven to 325º. Melt butter in 13 x 9 x 2 pan.

Roll potatoes in melted butter. Bake, uncovered, 1 hour; cut into quarters and season with the grilling salt; turn potatoes and add broth; bake another hour or until brown, turning several times.

Pass Creek Pasta

. . . .

Bob Richard

*This is one of my guests' favorites,
and a good backcountry food.*

Pasta, your choice
1/2 stick butter, browned
Ground pepper
Parmesan cheese

Boil pasta, drain. Place pasta in bowl. Add pepper and Parmesan cheese. Pour browned butter over the pasta.

Pierogi

· · · · · · · · · · · · · · · · · ·

Cheryl Jaworowski

Cheryl and pierogi are only two of Poland's many great exports.
Cheryl and her sister remember making pierogi between Thanksgiving and Christmas,
but they're good any time of year. In Whiting, Indiana, an annual festival is geared around
these delicious filled dumplings, which can be served as a side, main course, or if sweetened, as a dessert.

Dough:

> 3 cups flour
> 1 egg
> 1 teaspoon water
> 1 tablespoon butter
> 1 tablespoon oil

Place flour on a table. Make a well in the center; add egg and enough water to make a dough. Add butter and knead until dough is workable.

Fillings:

Be creative. Try the following options:

1. sauerkraut
2. mashed potatoes and sauerkraut, mixed together
3. mashed potatoes, cheddar cheese, and onions (fry the onions and mix with potatoes and cheese)
4. large-curd cottage cheese, farmer's cheese, and onions (fried), mixed together
5. cottage cheese or cream cheese with sugar added to taste

On a floured surface, roll out the dough; the thinner you can roll it, the more delicate the pierogi. Use a coffee cup to cut a circle. Place the filling of your choice onto one half of the circle. Wet the edges with water and fold the top half of the circle over the filling. Press to seal. Set the finished pierogi on a plate sprayed with nonstick spray.

Boil a pot of water with 1 tablespoon of oil. When water is boiling, place pierogi in boiling water. When they rise to the top, remove and drain. You can freeze, deep-fry, or eat them as they are with some sour cream and butter.

Refrigerator Coleslaw

· · · · · · · · · · · · · · · ·

Tom & Bonnie Murphy

This is also known as cabbage salad, or (in parts of Pennsylvania) pickled cabbage, a dish no self-respecting Pennsylvania Dutchman would leave off the dinner table. Use as a condiment with ham or other sliced meats, on sandwiches, or as a side dish.

> 1 medium head cabbage
> 1 medium carrot
> 1 green pepper
> 1 onion
> 1 teaspoon salt

Run all this through a food processor or chop finely by hand.

Dressing:

> 1 cup vinegar
> 1/4 cup water
> 2 cups sugar
> 1 teaspoon each celery seed and mustard seed

Combine dressing ingredients and boil for 1 minute. Cool to lukewarm and pour over the chopped vegetables. Put in quart jars in freezer or fridge—it makes 2 quarts.

Roosevelt Beans

· · · · · · · · · · · · · · · ·

ROOSEVELT LODGE
Chef Jim Chapman

1 pound hamburger or sausage
1/2 pound bacon, diced into half-inch pieces
1 onion, diced into half-inch pieces
1 can (16 ounces) pork and beans
1 can (12 ounces) kidney beans
1 can (12 ounces) lima beans
1 can (12 ounces) butter beans
1/2 cup brown sugar
2 tablespoons cider vinegar
1 tablespoon prepared mustard
1/2 cup ketchup
Salt and pepper to taste

Fry meats. Drain fat. Sauté onions with meat. Stir in remaining ingredients. (For a thicker product drain liquid from beans.) Bake at 325° for 45 minutes.

Yield 8 portions

Desserts

Antelope Toes

. . . .

Tom & Bonnie Murphy

This recipe came to me from David Offenbach of New York.
We actually like these better without the nuts. This recipe is easily doubled or tripled and
put in the freezer baked or raw. If you triple it you will always have them, even in the middle of the night.

3/4 cup butter or margarine
3/4 cup sugar
1 teaspoon vanilla extract
1 egg
2 cups flour
1/2 teaspoon salt
1 12-ounce package semisweet chocolate
    chips—preferably mini size
1 teaspoon shortening
Finely chopped nuts or sprinkles

Cream butter, sugar, vanilla, and egg until light. Mix flour and salt, and add to the first mix. Mix until well blended. Stir in 1/2 cup of the chocolate chips. Using 1 teaspoon per cookie, shape into log, and arrange on an ungreased cookie sheet. Bake in a 350° oven for 12 to 15 minutes per sheet; cool on wire racks.

Melt half the package of chocolate chips with the shortening.

When cookies are cool, dip half of each into the melted chocolate. Sprinkle with nuts or sprinkles. Let stand on wax paper until firm.

Apple Crisp

ROOSEVELT LODGE
Chef Jim Chapman

4 ounces butter
5 pounds sliced peeled apples
1 cup sugar
2 teaspoons cinnamon
$^1/_4$ teaspoon nutmeg
$^1/_4$ cup cornstarch
Crisp Topping, as needed

In a saucepan, melt butter; add all ingredients except topping. Bring to a simmer over medium heat, stirring occasionally. As mixture cooks it will begin to thicken. When desired consistency is reached, remove from heat and let cool.

Mixture may be used for individual servings in small ovenproof dishes, or in a baking pan. In either case spray vessel with cooking spray. Fill with apple mixture and top with crisp topping and bake until golden brown.

Crisp Topping:

$^3/_4$ pound butter
$^1/_2$ pound flour
10 ounces oats
1 pound brown sugar

Cream together sugar and butter, then fold in flour and oats. Mix should be fairly dry and crumbly.

Yield 15 portions

Banana Streusel Coffee Cake

Carolyn Wallen

1 cup flour, sifted
$1/2$ cup sugar
1 teaspoon baking powder
$1/2$ teaspoon salt
$1/4$ teaspoon baking soda
$1/8$ teaspoon fresh nutmeg, grated
$1/8$ teaspoon allspice, ground
2 medium bananas, ripe
1 egg, beaten
$1/4$ cup butter, melted and cooled
1 tablespoon milk
$1/2$ teaspoon vanilla
$1/2$ cup brown sugar, packed
3 tablespoons flour
$1/4$ teaspoon cinnamon
3 to 4 tablespoons butter, cold

Sift flour, then measure. Resift the flour along with the sugar, baking powder, salt, soda, nutmeg, and allspice.

In a small bowl, mash the bananas to make just under a cup.

In large mixing bowl, combine the mashed bananas, egg, butter, milk, and vanilla. Blend well; then add the dry ingredients to the banana mixture, mixing well.

Grease or butter an 8-inch round cake pan; pour half the batter mixture into the pan.

Prepare the streusel by combining the brown sugar, flour, and cinnamon in a small bowl. Cut in the butter until crumbly. Sprinkle half the streusel mixture over the batter in the pan.

Spoon on the remaining batter, covering the streusel. Sprinkle remaining crumbs over all.

Bake in 375° oven 25 to 30 minutes. Serve warm.

Boiling River Divinity

Jack & Tina Gilchrist

2¹/₂ cups sugar
¹/₂ cup corn syrup
¹/₂ cup water
¹/₃ teaspoon salt
2 egg whites
1 teaspoon vanilla
1 cup walnuts (optional)

In a 2-quart saucepan mix together sugar, corn syrup, water, and salt. Stirring constantly, bring to boil over medium heat. Reduce heat and cook WITHOUT stirring until temperature on candy thermometer reaches 248° or small amount dropped in very cold water forms a ball that does NOT flatten when removed from water.

Before temperature reaches 248°, in large bowl with mixer on high, beat whites until stiff peaks form. With mixer on high, SLOWLY pour about half the hot syrup over egg whites. Then cook remaining syrup to 272° or when a small amount dropped into very cold water separates into threads that are hard but not brittle.

Beating constantly, SLOWLY pour syrup over egg white mixture. Continue beating until mixture begins to lose its gloss and holds soft peaks when dropped from spoon. If mix becomes too stiff, beat with wooden spoon. Mix in vanilla and nuts, then drop by teaspoonfuls onto wax paper. Work quickly because candy sets up as it cools.

Yields 1¹/₄ pounds or 48 pieces

Brown Sugar Cookies

Barbara Forbes Rinker

These cookies were sent to us by my roommate's mother, Reba Carlson, when we worked at Fishing Bridge. They were greatly appreciated! (Barbara maintains a web page with wonderful old photos of her savage days: www.bill.rinker.net/yellowstone.htm.)

Mix:

1 1/2 cups brown sugar
3 cups flour
3 eggs
1 cup Crisco

Add:

1 teaspoon baking soda in 1/4 cup hot water
1 teaspoon baking powder
1/2 cup cocoa
1 teaspoon salt
Chopped nuts (optional)

Bake 350° for 8 to 10 minutes.

Ice with powdered sugar icing, if desired.

Barbara Forbes Rinker, A Park Savage at Heart

I n 1951 Barbara Forbes Rinker was a savage, and she couldn't have been happier. It doesn't seem fitting that this quiet midwesterner should be saddled with such a vicious moniker, but political correctness wasn't an issue then. In fact, all Yellowstone concessionaire employees were referred to as savages. "It was part of the park lingo," Barbara says. "Tourists were dudes, dishwashers were pearl divers, and bus drivers were gear jammers."*

Barbara earned her nickname while in college. To get out of Indiana during summer break, she and a sorority sister wrote to several places. "Yellowstone said if we could be there in 10 days we could have the job—it's not that easy anymore," she notes. By her third summer she had worked her way from bus girl in the cafeteria at Fishing Bridge to waitress at Lake Lodge, where she often made $100 a day in tips—in silver dollars. "People were on vacation, you got to know them, and they tipped well."

Lake Lodge savages had to help with nightly entertainment for the dudes. "I played the piano and my roommate sang. Another friend, Paul Boehner, wrote a musical about Yellowstone, including songs about Fishing Bridge and life there. His work is housed in the park archives." For Christmas in Yellowstone (always in August) Barbara was part of Handel's *Messiah*—"a big production." On the less theatrical side, all the waitresses would sing Yellowstone songs to the tourists before they entered the dining hall. "If they were eating, we'd go to their table and sing, 'We're sorry you're going away….' They loved it and of course it helped with the tips."

Entertainment for the savages consisted of going to a movie or a nearby town, but because none of them had cars, hitchhiking was customary. "The rangers said it was safer to go with a family but to be cautious—it really wasn't a problem in those days." One trip took Barbara and two friends to Red Lodge for buffalo burgers.

It began to snow and cars on the road were few, so the restaurant owners made them a sign, which got them picked up by a man shipping out to the war in Korea. "I don't think he cared whether he lived or died. We were terrified as we flew over all the switchbacks."

Over the years the savages have been holding reunions at Lake Hotel and Lake Lodge, hosting about 50 ex-employees each year. Barbara says, "It's always amazing to find how many couples had met there and gotten married." Although she wasn't one of them, her husband heard so much about Yellowstone from her that he brought the family to the park to camp. They bought property nearby and finally retired near the entrance to Grand Teton.

Barbara was part of Yellowstone during an exciting, wonderful, even romantic era that only a relatively few people experienced. It was happy days, a time of family values, respect for others, and decorum—and she was a savage.

The book A Yellowstone Savage *by Joyce Lohse identifies these and other terms as well as their origins.*

Recipes by Barbara Forbes Rinker

Chocolate Dream Squares

Lee Whittlesey

20 graham crackers, crushed fine
$1/2$ pound butter, or margarine
2 cups powdered sugar
3 eggs
3 squares of bitter chocolate, melted
   but slightly cool
$1^1/2$ cups chopped nuts
1 teaspoon vanilla

Line an 8-inch square pan with half of graham cracker crumbs. Cream butter (or margarine) and powdered sugar. Beat in eggs one at a time. Beat in chocolate. Stir in nuts and vanilla.

Spread mixture into pan and sprinkle top with remaining graham cracker crumbs.

Refrigerate overnight. Serve on individual plates, topped with ice cream if desired.

Chocolate Pecan Rum Pie

· · · · · · · · · · · · · · · · · ·

Tara Cross & David Monteith

For added flavor in the piecrust, add 1 tablespoon sugar and replace 2 tablespoons water with raspberry vinegar. The crust will brown more quickly, so cover edges for the first part of the baking process.

2 ounces unsweetened chocolate
1 cup sugar
1 cup light corn syrup
4 tablespoons butter
Pinch of salt
3 tablespoons rum
1 teaspoon vanilla
3 eggs, lightly beaten
2 cups pecan halves
Piecrust for 1 pie

Preheat oven to 375º. In medium saucepan, melt chocolate, sugar, corn syrup, butter, and salt over low heat. Add rum and vanilla and let cool. Stir in eggs (do not overbeat eggs). Place nuts in piecrust; pour chocolate mixture over top. Bake for 15 minutes, then reduce heat to 325º and bake for 30 to 40 minutes longer, until filling is set. Serve at room temperature with whipped cream or ice cream if desired.

Chow Mein Chewies

Barbara Forbes Rinker

These were made every Christmas by my third graders in Haley Elementary,
Fort Wayne, Indiana. Quite a chore for a roomful of 26 kids.

1 six-ounce package butterscotch chips
1 six-ounce package chocolate chips
1 can chow mein noodles
1 cup chopped nuts

Melt chips in double boiler over boiling water, stirring occasionally. Remove from heat and stir in chow mein noodles and nuts. Drop by teaspoons onto wax paper.

Crème Caramel

. . . .

OLD FAITHFUL SNOW LODGE
Chef Jim Chapman

2¹/₂ cups granulated sugar
¹/₄ teaspoon water
¹/₂ tablespoon lemon juice
3 cups milk
1¹/₄ cups whole eggs
¹/₄ cup egg yolks
1 tablespoon vanilla extract

In a small saucepan combine 1 cup sugar, water, and lemon juice. Bring to a boil and cook until mixture turns golden brown. Pour an equal amount of caramel into 10, 4-ounce ceramic ramekins.

In another saucepan combine milk, ³/₄ cup sugar, and vanilla; bring to boil. While heating milk whip remaining ³/₄ cup sugar with eggs and yolks. When milk boils, remove from heat, very slowly add milk to eggs while constantly stirring.

Place ramekins with caramel into baking pan and fill ³/₄ of the way with custard mixture. Place pan in 325° oven. Fill pan with hot water, immersing ramekins halfway with water. Bake until fully set 25 to 30 minutes. Remove ramekins from pan, let cool slightly, then individually wrap with plastic wrap and cool overnight in refrigerator.

Unmold custard from ramekins by running a paring knife around cup, loosening custard from ramekin and upending onto plate. Serve with fresh fruit garnish and whipped cream.

Yield 10 portions

Gladys's Chocolate Chip Cookies

. . . .

Cheryl Jaworowski

My mother-in-law taught me how to use fructose in baking.
Fructose is metabolized more slowly than sugar and causes less of a spike in blood glucose than refined sugar, which is important to me because I'm hypoglycemic. Use less fructose than regular sugar and bake these cookies at 25 degrees less than you normally would.
Fructose chocolate chip cookies are soft and chewy. These cookies are a favorite among family and friends.

2¹/₂ cups unbleached Hungarian high-altitude
   flour (all purpose will work, too)
1 teaspoon baking soda
1 teaspoon salt
2 sticks of margarine
1 cup fructose
2 large eggs
1 teaspoon vanilla extract
1 package chocolate chips

Preheat oven to 350°.

Mix flour, baking soda, and salt together, and set aside. In a separate bowl, mix margarine with fructose until creamy. Add eggs and beat the mixture again. Scrape sides of bowl to ensure an even mixture, add vanilla extract, and beat. Add dry ingredients and beat mixture until creamy. Add chocolate chips and mix.

Use a teaspoon to place cookie dough on cookie sheets and bake 10 to 15 minutes or until golden brown. Fructose cookies brown easily, so you may need to move cookie sheets if your oven does not bake evenly.

Grammy's Rhubarb Pie

. . . .

Jennifer Whipple

This rhubarb pie with a meringue top is a favorite of mine that my grandmother always had waiting when my family visited in the spring. The recipe has that marvelous old-fashioned "mix a little of this and that" feel that reflected Grammy's amazing ability to conjure up a great result while not measuring anything, just tasting when appropriate.

3 or slightly more cups cut uncooked rhubarb
  (the old-fashioned green type is best)
1 1/4 cups sugar
4 tablespoons flour
3 eggs, separated

Combine all but 1/2 cup of the sugar with the rhubarb. Combine the flour with the remaining sugar and add to rhubarb along with the 3 egg yolks. Mix, then let mixture stand until juicy. Put into 8-inch piecrust (unbaked), and bake in 400° oven. When crust is beginning to brown, cover top of pie with pie pan until rhubarb cooks. Take out of the oven.

Meanwhile, make a meringue with the egg whites. Cover the pie with the meringue and bake until meringue is lightly browned.

Honey Bits

* * * * * * * * * * * * * * * * * * * *

Lee Whittlesey

1/2 cup honey
1/2 cup peanut butter
1 cup dry milk

Mix thoroughly. Knead until shiny. Roll into small balls.

Jelly Roll

* * * * * * * * * * * * * * * * * * * *

Lee Whittlesey

3 eggs
1 cup sugar
5 tablespoons water
1 teaspoon vanilla
1 cup flour
1 teaspoon baking powder
1/2 teaspoon salt
Jelly, your choice

Beat thoroughly eggs and sugar. Add water and vanilla. Mix flour, baking powder, and salt. Add dry ingredients; do not overbeat.

Use a nonstick pan, or grease a jelly roll pan, line it with wax paper or parchment, then grease the paper. Pour in batter and bake at 350º for 10 to 15 minutes, until cake springs back when touched.

Invert cake onto another piece of parchment or wax paper, spread with jelly, and roll up tightly, using the paper to help you get started. Lay roll seam side down until completely cool and it retains its shape. You can sift powdered sugar or leave it plain. Cut into slices.

Monster Cookies

· · · · · · · · · · · · · · · · · ·

Tom & Bonnie Murphy

These are considered survival food in the Rockies. A couple in your pack and you can go all day. These are every bit as good as those that are sold commercially—good thing, too, because the recipe makes a huge batch. Of course, you can cut it in half but it freezes so well you might as well make them all. The recipe was taken from the Livingston Enterprise *newspaper.*

NOTE: *Read carefully before you begin, and use a very large bowl.*

- 2 pounds brown sugar
- 4 cups white sugar (can decrease this a little if you want a less sweet cookie)
- 1 pound margarine (not soft type)
- 1 dozen eggs
- 2.8-pound jar peanut butter
- 1 tablespoon vanilla
- 1 tablespoon corn syrup
- 8 teaspoons baking soda
- 18 cups quick oatmeal
- 2 cups walnuts or pecans, coarsely chopped
- 2 12-ounce packages chocolate chips
- 1 box raisins (optional)

Mix together sugars, margarine, and eggs with electric mixer or by hand until thoroughly blended. Add peanut butter, vanilla, corn syrup, and baking soda, and mix well. Then add oatmeal, nuts, and chocolate chips. There is no flour in this dough, so it is sticky. Form into patties about 3 inches across and $1/2$ inch thick. Place cookies on a well-greased cookie sheet and bake at 350º for about 15 minutes. They will look puffy and like they aren't quite done but they are best this way. Leave them on the cookie sheet until they firm up, then dry on racks until cool.

To keep in the freezer, divide the raw dough into about 8 batches and put into plastic containers or freezer bags. Remove from the freezer the night before you need a batch, then bake like fresh dough.

Mother's White Fudge

Barbara Forbes Rinker

My Mother, Letha Forbes, was known for this delicious fudge every holiday.
We all try to make it at Christmas.

3 cups sugar (cane sugar only)
1/2 teaspoon salt
1 stick butter
1 cup milk
2 tablespoons light Karo syrup
1 teaspoon vanilla

Combine the sugar, salt, butter, milk, and Karo syrup in heavy pan. Stir until it boils at 220°. Stop stirring and continue to cook until it forms a firm ball in cold water. Add vanilla. Cool over cold water; do not stir. Then beat until it is thick, and quickly put into a buttered pan.

Mrs. Burns's Lemon Pie

Jack & Tina Gilchrist

This is one of those recipes that can get renamed every time it's passed on.
It goes great with baked beans on Saturday night, a Depression Era meal.

1 cup sugar
5 tablespoons cornstarch
¼ teaspoon salt

Mix together and pour over this:

2 cups boiling water

Cook until thick and add:

3 tablespoons lemon juice
2 egg yolks

Cool slightly and spoon into baked piecrust.

Meringue:

2 egg whites well beaten
3 tablespoons sugar

Slowly add sugar to egg whites and beat, beat, and beat until stiff peaks form.

Top pie with meringue and put under broiler until slightly brown.

No Bake Cookies

. . . .

Ruth and Leslie Quinn

*Do not attempt to double this recipe because
the mixture may harden before you can get all the cookies dropped.*

1 stick margarine or butter
2 cups sugar
$^1/_2$ cup milk
$^1/_4$ cup cocoa
3 cups oatmeal
1 teaspoon vanilla
$^1/_2$ cup peanut butter
Pinch of salt

Melt the butter in a 3-quart saucepan. Add sugar, milk, and cocoa. Bring this mixture to a boil and boil for 1 minute. Remove from heat. Immediately stir in oatmeal, vanilla, peanut butter, and salt until blended. Drop onto wax paper with a small spoon. Cookies will become firm as they cool. Eat and store when cool.

Old Faithful Inn Delight Cake

· · · · · · · · · · · · · · · · · ·

Dianna Kellie

3 cups flour
1/2 cup baking cocoa
1 3/4 cups sugar
3 teaspoons baking powder
3/4 teaspoon baking soda
3/4 cup butter, room temperature
1 3/4 cups milk
3 eggs
1 1/2 teaspoons vanilla
1/4 teaspoon cinnamon

Mix all dry ingredients in bowl. Add other ingredients and mix for 2 minutes on medium speed. Pour into a 9 x 13 pan and bake at 350° for 30 to 40 minutes. Baking times for different ovens vary, so check cake often. Ice with huckleberry icing.

Buttercreme Huckleberry Icing for Old Faithful Inn Delight Cake

From huckleberry chocolates to huckleberry-scented hand lotion, ice cream, and jam, huckleberries are a western Montana staple. Dianna notes that if you want to use this icing for decorating, omit the jam because it doesn't work well in cake-decorating tubes.

1/3 cup water
2 tablespoons meringue powder
6 cups confectioners sugar, sifted (1 1/2 pounds)
3/4 cup solid shortening
dash salt
1/2 teaspoon almond flavoring
1/2 teaspoon clear vanilla flavoring
1/8 teaspoon butter flavoring
1/4 cup or so huckleberry jam

Combine water and meringue powder; whip at high speed until peaks form. Add 2 cups of sugar, 1 at a time, beating after each addition at low speed. Add alternately, shortening and rest of sugar; add salt and flavorings. Add huckleberry jam according to taste.

Yields approximately 3 1/2 cups

Dianna Kellie; She Loves the Inn

The license plate on Dianna Kellie's car reads LUV OFI—translation, Love Old Faithful Inn, a huge under-statement. Her love affair with the park's most famous building began in room 2002 on her birthday in 1997. "I hadn't been in the park for a while, and to treat myself I requested the best suite they had at the inn. That's all it took. I thought, this is a fabulous place and I have to learn more about it." Wondering what other rooms might be like, Dianna decided to make it a goal to stay in every one of the inn's original 93 rooms, and she's gaining. She books a year in advance to try to snag the accommodations she wants.

"I love the old house's outdoorsy look. It's not like walking into an institutional place like a chain motel; it's more like being home." Dianna highly recommends room number 229, a great balcony room; room 150 allows a wonderful geyser view; 46 is good; 54 is good—"they're all basically good." The backside rooms don't have the views, but they're still worthy of a stay. "People might complain about it but I almost hate to see the cantankerous heating system replaced—it adds to the inn's character."

Old Faithful Inn holds many secrets and trivial information that most visitors, even its architect/designer Robert Reamer aren't aware of, such as:

- There are numerous signatures all over the building, many hidden. For example, on one of the upper logs in room 46 is artist Charles Russell's signature—"I need to photograph that," Dianna notes.
- Until 1946, the inn had nickel pay toilets.
- Room 117 is called the mystery room, not because of anything creepy but because of its carpet. "It's unique to that room. It's not in any other place in the inn and too hideous for the rest of the building. It's a mystery why it's there," Dianna says.
- On a drawer in one room is 80 years' worth of names and dates.
- People claim they've seen the ghost of the third floor. "It's supposed to be someone's

wedding night and the bride died; others claim it's Reamer, but I think it's just a story."
• The inn has 327 rooms (before renovation) counting east and west wings.

With her insider knowledge and devotion to the building, who better to serve as master of ceremonies for the inn's 100-year celebration in 2004? Dianna wrote and presented a tribute to the inn that was fitting of a Hollywood celebrity.

Devotees tend to be collectors, so it's no surprise that Dianna has plans to accumulate the largest collection of inn memorabilia. One of her hundreds of postcards stands out: "On it, Reamer drew the inn during its construction and signed Old Faithful Inn on the front. It's in mint condition." Another equally rare treasure is a glass slide of a room that is no longer there or has been drastically altered.

Memorial Day weekend (and June and July and…) finds Dianna content at Old Faithful Inn. "I love it there—it's my heaven on earth."

Recipes by Dianna Kellie

Passion Chocolate Cake

. . . .

Tom & Bonnie Murphy

This recipe is from Oasa Murphy, Tom's mother. The reason we call it Passion Chocolate Cake is that one time when Tom and I lived in the Black Hills, we had a terrible three-day blizzard and we had run out of cocoa, so Tom (an admitted chocoholic) walked to the grocery store to get it so we could make the cake. As he walked out into the storm and disappeared after about a minute, I thought, "This guy really has a passion for chocolate." We renamed the cake when he got home.

1 cup flour
3/4 cup sugar
1/2 teaspoon salt
2 teaspoons baking powder
2 tablespoons cocoa
2 tablespoons butter
1/2 cup milk
1 teaspoon vanilla

Beat well and pour into 8 x 8 glass baking dish.

Mix and spread over the top:
    1/2 cup white sugar
    1/2 cup brown sugar
    2 tablespoons cocoa
    1 cup hot water

Bake at 350º for 30 minutes. Serve with fresh cream.

Pear Crisp

. . . .

Suzanne Lewis

*This recipe is from my friend
who had two pear trees in her yard and
needed to create something to use the pears.*

5 large pears
1 teaspoon cinnamon
1 teaspoon nutmeg
1 tablespoon lemon juice
$1/2$ cup water
1 cup sugar
$3/4$ cup flour
$1/2$ cup butter or margarine

Peel and slice pears into buttered baking dish;
sprinkle with spices. Add lemon juice to water and
pour over pears. Mix flour and sugar. Cut in butter
to make crumbly mixture. Spoon over pears.

Bake uncovered for 1 hour at 350°.

Pecan Cookies

. . . .

Tara Cross & David Monteith

This is simple but delicious!

$1/2$ cup brown sugar
2 tablespoons sugar
1 cup butter (or $1/2$ cup butter, $1/2$ cup margarine)
1 egg, separated
2 cups flour
36 pecan halves

Cream sugars, butter, and egg yolk. Mix in flour
to form dough.

Roll dough into balls; dip fork in egg white and
press down. Place pecan half on each cookie. Bake
at 350°, watching after 7 to 8 minutes.

Makes 36 cookies

Pineapple Carrot Cake

Suzanne Lewis

2 cups flour, presifted
1 1/2 cups sugar
1 teaspoon baking soda
2 teaspoons cinnamon
1/2 teaspoon salt
3 eggs
1/2 cup oil
3/4 cup buttermilk
1 teaspoon vanilla
2 cans (8 1/2 ounces) crushed pineapple, drained
2 cups shredded carrots, packed
1 cup chopped walnuts

Mix flour, sugar, baking soda, cinnamon, and salt. Beat eggs with oil, buttermilk, and vanilla. Add dry ingredients all at once to wet mixture. Mix in pineapple and carrots and nuts. Bake in a well-greased and floured pan (9 x 13 or tube pan) at 350º for 45 to 55 minutes. Ice if desired.

Rescue Cookies

Joe Bueter

These are often served at "staff meetings" in Joe and Juanita's kitchen.

1 cup margarine
1¹/₄ cups brown sugar
¹/₂ cup sugar
2 eggs
2 tablespoons milk
2 teaspoons vanilla
2 cups flour
1 teaspoon baking soda
¹/₂ teaspoon salt
3 cups quick-cooking oats
¹/₄ teaspoon nutmeg
1 teaspoon cinnamon

Beat together margarine, brown sugar, and sugar. Add eggs, milk, and vanilla, and mix well. Add the combined mixture of flour, baking soda, salt, and quick-cooking oats, nutmeg, and cinnamon. Bake at 375° for 9 or 10 minutes.

Joe Bueter, A Ranger's Ranger

Although his official title is park ranger, he's much more than the stereotype waving people through the entrance gate, although he occasionally helps with that, too. Mostly Joe Bueter is a ranger/paramedic/police officer—no way to shorten the title or what it involves. All rangers are emergency medical technicians (EMTs), but Joe is the highest level, attained after 1,500 hours of training.

Joe's typical summer day can include directing traffic at an animal jam, answering a medical call, and making arrests: mostly for DUI, drugs, and assault. "I've arrested one person about every one to two weeks," Joe says. "Basically after 5 PM if there's a problem, it's my problem."

Most EMT incidents are strokes and heart attacks. "We do what paramedics do in every city in the country," Joe says. "The things that make the paper here are gorings, maulings, and scaldings." Joe's been here since 1989 with only one bear mauling—and that was outside the park. In the winter the majority of his calls are snowmobile accidents around Cooke City.

Park visitors aren't restricted to staying on trails except in thermal areas, and it's not uncommon for a hiker to get lost because of the park's accessibility. So Joe helps find them. Not all searches turn out well, however. He says the most disturbing incident was a triple (three people) burn in a thermal feature in which three teenagers hopped over features on a trail at night. They misjudged a drainage and landed in a 30-foot-deep hot pool, burning 97 percent of their bodies. One died.

Emergency medical service in the park isn't all about the big wrecks. "We certainly have them but we deal with people on a broader sense," Joe says. For example, a husband has a heart attack and dies, and the widow is stuck all alone in a strange place with an RV that she can't drive. "So we step in," Joe says. "We clean the food out of the fridge in the Winnebago, get the survivor to the airport, and take care of the pet dog— whatever it takes."

He means it. He tells of a woman who had end-stage cancer. Her children brought her to the park as a last get-together but she fell ill in her room. The daughter called Joe. The family hadn't realized that at 7,000 feet in elevation even healthy people would have trouble breathing. With Joe's help the woman got better and made it back home. "Joe came home, slept a few hours, then went back to check on her. This is the core of what he does," says his wife, Juanita, the school nurse at Mammoth.

Joe and his coworkers are the heart of the park—he can arrest you, warn you, and save your life, but he hopes he never needs to. However, with three million-plus visitors a year coming to Yellowstone, Joe's not likely to be out of a job anytime soon.

Recipes by Joe Bueter

Rick's Chocolate Chip Cookies

Jennifer Whipple

These cookies were my late husband's (park geologist Rick Hutchinson) absolute favorite cookie, and he regularly worked his way through a batch of them every week! The recipe is modified for the high elevation at Old Faithful (7,000 feet) but will work at lower elevations.

1½ cups brown sugar
   (a little less at Old Faithful)
1 cup butter
2 eggs
2 teaspoons real vanilla extract
2 cups + 5 tablespoons flour
   (a heaping ¼ cup measure)
½ teaspoon baking soda
½ teaspoon salt
1¼ cups chopped walnuts
12 ounces bittersweet or
   semisweet chocolate chips

Preheat oven to 375º for shiny metal cookie sheet.

In a mixing bowl, cream the brown sugar, butter, eggs, and vanilla. Sift the flour, baking soda, and salt together, and slowly stir into the batter until thoroughly mixed and smooth. Add the walnuts and chocolate chips, and mix.

Drop the batter from a teaspoon well apart on a cookie sheet and bake for 8 to 10 minutes.

Sugar Cookies

Dianna Kellie

1 1/2 cups powdered sugar
1 cup butter or margarine, softened
1 teaspoon real vanilla
1 teaspoon almond extract
1 large egg
2 1/2 cups flour
1 teaspoon baking soda
1 teaspoon cream of tartar
Cookie sprinkles

Heat oven to 370°.

Mix powdered sugar, butter, vanilla, almond extract, and egg. Stir in remaining ingredients. Cover and refrigerate for 3 hours. Divide dough into halves. Roll each half to $^3/_{16}$ inch or so on lightly floured board. Cut into various shapes with cookie cutters. Top with cookie sprinkles; place on lightly greased cookie sheet.

Bake until edges are light brown, about 7 to 8 minutes.

Makes approximately 4 1/2 dozen cookies

Sunlight Lemon Pie

· · · · · · · · · · · · · · · · · · ·

Bob Richard
I always double this recipe—it's that good.

1 9-inch piecrust
   (can use purchased frozen crust)
1 cup sugar
3 tablespoons cornstarch
4 tablespoons butter
3 large egg yolks, beaten
1 cup whole milk
1 teaspoon fresh grated lemon peel
1/4 cup lemon juice
1 cup sour cream
Sweetened whipped cream
Sugared lemon slices
Chopped walnuts

Bake piecrust.

In saucepan, mix sugar, cornstarch, butter, egg yolks, and milk. Stir and cook until thick, 5 to 10 minutes. Add lemon peel and lemon juice. Cool. Fold in sour cream. Pour into piecrust and refrigerate overnight

Top with whipped cream, lemon slices, and chopped walnuts.

Super Easy Peanut Butter Cookies

Carl Sheehan

1 cup sugar
1 cup peanut butter
1 egg

Optional: $^1/_2$ cup chopped walnuts (if adding walnuts, also add a bit more peanut butter)

Preheat oven to 375°

Mix, sugar, peanut butter, and egg. Roll into 1-inch balls; flatten with fork. Bake for 12 minutes or until light golden brown.

Makes 1 dozen

Whistle Creek Almond Roca

. . . .

Bob Richard

Bob says this is an old recipe, so adjust chocolate bar prices/sizes accordingly.
The heat of the mixture will melt the chocolate bars. Dark or milk chocolate will work.

$1/2$ pound butter
1 cup sugar (rounded)
3 tablespoons Karo syrup (dark or light)
1 tablespoon water
1 cup almonds, chopped
Chocolate bars (see directions)

Combine butter, sugar, Karo syrup, and water, cook in heavy skillet until it smokes or forms hard brittle ball in cold water. Sprinkle $1/2$ cup chopped almonds on a buttered cookie sheet. Pour candy mixture over nuts, spread, and cover with five 5-cent Hershey bars (or one 50-cent bar); spread chocolate and sprinkle remaining almonds over top (the heat of the mixture will melt the chocolate bars). Cool and break out of pan.

Keep refrigerated.

Sauces & Dressings

Asian Honey Mustard Dressing

Tara Cross & David Monteith

2 cloves garlic
$1/3$ cup honey
$1/4$ cup Dijon mustard
2 tablespoons lemon juice
$1/4$ cup rice vinegar
1 cup peanut oil
$1/2$ teaspoon dark sesame oil

In blender or food processor, puree garlic. Combine with honey, mustard, lemon juice, and vinegar; mix 1 minute. Add oils slowly with motor running. Process until smooth and creamy. Store in refrigerator.

Big Bear's Pizza Sauce

Carl Sheehan
Carl says for the best crust, bake it on a pizza stone.

1 can (28 ounces) tomatoes, whole,
   peeled and drained
1 can (16 ounces) tomato sauce
Dash or two of wine/beer
1 tablespoon garlic powder (or 8 cloves,
   chopped)
1 tablespoon onion salt (or 1 medium onion,
   chopped)
1 tablespoon oregano
1 tablespoon powdered fennel seed (or whole)
1 tablespoon brown sugar
1 tablespoon Parmesan cheese
1/2 teaspoon ground hot chili pepper (or less)
1/2 teaspoon mustard powder
More oregano
Dash of bay leaf, ground
Dash of basil, sweet
Dash of cinnamon
Dash of honey

Your favorite pizza crust

Combine all ingredients and simmer several hours (the longer the better). Keep tasting and adding more. Remember that it should taste strong—it will be spread thin on a lot of crust.

Optional additions: onions, pepper, mushrooms, pineapple bits, shrimp, trout, peanut butter, bananas, sauerkraut...

Bake pizza at 500° until golden brown (15-20 minutes).

Hollandaise Sauce

. . . .

Bob Richard

1/4 pound butter
1/2 teaspoon Worcestershire sauce
4 egg yolks
Salt
Pepper
1/4 teaspoon dry mustard
1/2 cup boiling water
2 to 3 tablespoons lemon juice

Mix butter, Worcestershire sauce, egg yolks, salt, pepper, and mustard until smooth. Put in double boiler and add boiling water. Stir constantly until it starts to thicken and sticks to end of a tablespoon. Don't overcook. Remove and add lemon juice.

Pour over vegetables and serve.

Recipes by contributor

About the author

Like the people in *The Yellowstone National Park Cookbook*, Durrae Johanek fell in love with Montana, Yellowstone, and the West in general. She and her husband, John, moved from Pennsylvania to Big Sky Country in 1992. They spent years taking in the sights and scenery, then writing down their discoveries in two books: *Montana Behind the Scenes* and *Montana Folks*.

A graduate of Kutztown University, Pennsylvania, Durrae grew up in Pennsylvania Dutch country, a land of strange and unpronounceable foods, but she is a food-ophile nonetheless. She can be found at the Cafe Zydeco in Bozeman or "over the hill" in Livingston at Adagio, happily downing her favorite fare and unabashedly begging a recipe or two.